Zreda Herther,
from RobertaSm
W9-CJI-882

You're From ...Where?

Robert T. Smith
Illustrations by Denise Macko

Voyageur Press

Text copyright © 1991 by Robert T. Smith
Illustrations copyright © 1991 by Denise Macko

All rights reserved. No part of this work may be repro-
duced or used in any form by any means--graphic,
electronic, or mechanical, including photocopying,
recording, taping, or any information storage and
retrieval system--without written permission of the
publisher.

Printed in the United States of America
91 92 93 94 95 5 4 3 2 1

Library of Congress Cataloging-in-Publication Data

Smith, Robert T., 1925-
    You're from where? / Robert T. Smith.
        p. cm.
    ISBN 0-89658-146-2
    1. Names, Geographical -- United States -- Humor.
2. United States -- History, Local -- Humor. I. Title.
E155.S65 1991
973--dc20   91-9318
                                                  CIP

Published by
Voyageur Press, Inc.
P.O. Box 338
123 North Second Street
Stillwater, MN 55082 U.S.A.
In Minn 612-430-2210
Toll-free 800-888-9653

Voyageur Press books are also available at discounts for
quantities for educational, fundraising, premium, or
sales-promotion use. For details contact the marketing
department. Please write or call for our free catalog of
publications.

CONTENTS

DEDICATION

This book could not have been written without generous assistance from residents of the small towns included herein. Those stories that were chosen are listed at the end of the book with the contributors' names; information received without a sender's name is attributed to Anonymous.

To the several newspapers that gave my stories exposure in a weekly column, a special thanks for the encouragement they offered. They are the *Rochester* (Minnesota) *Post-Bulletin*, the *Green Bay* (Wisconsin) *Press-Gazette*, the *Citrus County* (Florida) *Chronicle*, the *Fort Myers* (Florida) *News-Press*, the *Sebring* (Florida) *News-Sun*, and the Leesburg (Florida) *Daily Commercial*.

Also, a great big thank you to my long-suffering best friend, grammar-straightener-outer, chief menu-planner, best friend, champion of my health, rewriter extraordinaire, best friend, loving companion, calmer-downer, best friend, family financial planner and bookkeeper, laugher at my sometimes dumb jokes, best friend, listener to my problems, the one who sides with me (sometimes even when I'm wrong) in any dispute, best friend, world-class good scout, vetoer of my more inane ideas, resident sweetie-pie, best friend--and wife, Mary Torrison-Smith.

INTRODUCTION

This book of odd and unusual place names in the United States has many authors. They are the hundreds of small-town residents who responded to my inquiring postcard with such generosity of spirit and such an outpouring of fascinating information that the post office of the small town where I live was a lively place for months. I was inundated with postcards, letters, newspaper clippings, maps, leaflets, and local history books. For months my daily walk through town to pick up the mail became an adventure, with new treasures of recollections and reminiscences stuffed into my post office box, waiting to be savored and sifted into this compilation. Discovering how Moon, Virginia; Soso, Mississippi; Nameless, Tennessee; Toad Hop, Indiana; Embarrass, Wisconsin; Tightwad, Missouri; and so many others acquired their names became a daily delight.

These consistently warm and generous responses to a stranger's inquiry came from Americans in hundred of communities throughout the land, from Maine to California, Florida to Alaska, with all states represented. These mailings have generated in me new appreciation for my country and its men and women. I gained new respect and affection for these present-day residents of America's small communities and for those still-remembered founders and namers whose stories you are about to read. Their stories are tales of the settling of our vast land.

Some of the names you may recognize: Death Valley, California; Ten Sleep, Wyoming; and Horseheads, New York are among them. But names like Lulu, Florida; Round O, South Carolina; Turkey Scratch, Arkansas; and Old Glory, Texas, highlight the reality that we don't all live in Chicago, Miami, Minneapolis, Los Angeles, or New York City.

We know that settlement of our nation began in the sixteenth, seventeenth, and eighteenth centuries with the Spanish, Dutch, English, and French settlers who brought their cultures and their place names to our country. As the colonists arrived in the New England area, they evidently needed to bring a little bit of England with them. Thus many settlements, particularly in Massachusetts, were given the names of the English towns or people left behind. Bath, London, and Manchester are a few examples.

As pioneers moved westward, they often took their towns' names with them. Sandwich, Illinois, was settled by people from the Massachusetts Sandwich; Climax, Kansas, was named by a settler for his former hometown, Climax, Michigan.

Many Indian place names were usurped along with their land. Germans, Scandinavians, Italians, and eastern Europeans arrived during the nineteenth and twentieth centuries, planting new settlements across the continent. Most of the unusual place names arrived during the expansion beyond the original thirteen colonies through the south and west.

Who were these people? Who were these adventurous souls who courageously pushed on into virgin territory, alone or in caravans of covered wagons, on foot, by riverboat, and later by train?

These transplanted Americans were fishermen and smugglers, fur trappers and farmers, loggers and railroad builders, miners and oil drillers. They came as explorers and cowboys, clergy members and outlaws, optimists and cynics, the rich and the desperately poor. They included the holders of giant land grants and the landless, aristocrats and slaves, skilled artisans, soldiers, scholars, debtors, and many children.

Many communities with delightful names were quickly settled. They grew as boom towns, almost from the dust, thanks to the advent of railroads, logging camps, mining operations, oil drilling, and so on. Then, just as quickly, the majority reverted to the "wide place in the road" that they are today. Some populations have been reduced to fewer than five, and most to five hundred or fewer. Other communities grew and remain today as small thriving cities.

For the most part, we opt for short, easily pronounced town names. The U.S. Postal Service (and its earlier incarnation, the Post Office Department) has, at times, applied pressure, ranging from friendly persuasion to outright veto, to encourage a town to select a brief name. Few other countries share this approach. The most famous example is the town in Wales called Llanfairpwyllgwyngyllgogerychwymdrobwillllantysiliogogogoch. Enough said.

Some towns used the device of reverse spelling, often that of the name of a founder. If there already was a town in the state with the desired name, residents often spelled the name backward to "keep it in the family." For example, Reklaw, Texas, was derived from the name Walker, an early pioneer in the town. Remlap, Alabama is a reversal of Palmer. And Remlig, Texas was named for a local businessman, Alexander Gilmer.

A railroad official got into the act in Oregon. There the town of Retlaw was named by the railroad after H. L. Walter. Governor Ernest Lister was honored with the reverse spelling of his name in Retsil, Washington. Towns were remembered in this way as well. Wabasso, Florida, was named by founders who relocated from Ossabaw, Georgia, and wanted to take a little bit of home with them.

Usually any hint of smallness was avoided; but Micro, North Carolina, and Iota, Louisiana, are exceptions. And, although many early settlers steered away from unpleasant names, frustrations were reflected in town names like Hell, Michigan; Lick Skillet, Ohio; and Hardscrabble in many states. The flip side of the coin gave us the upbeat names of Hope, New Jersey; Nobility, Texas; Future City, Illinois; and Fairdealing, Missouri.

Many towns will beckon from the pages of this book. Many more remain by the side of the road for lack of space to include them. And you may know different stories behind some of the names. I invite you to explore the byways of our country, starting with this look at the hope and humor that was, and is, America.

ACCORD, MASSACHUSETTS

More than likely, what they all *really* wanted was to get in out of the cold.

This small community in eastern Massachusetts, thirty miles southeast of the state capital of Boston, was once the site of negotiations between early settlers and a local Native American tribe. Meeting upon a frozen pond one cold Massachusetts winter day, the groups didn't take long to reach an accord, sign a treaty, and head for home.

The pond promptly became Accord Pond, and its neighbors have lived in Accord ever since.

Located fifteen miles west of the Atlantic Ocean, Accord abuts two other towns, still rubbing its civic shoulders in harmonious accord.

ALADDIN, WYOMING

Once upon a time, long before this town in Wyoming was settled, Scheherazade, the legendary storyteller of the "Arabian Nights," told the tale of Aladdin.

As a youth, Aladdin was sent into a cave to retrieve a lamp. When he accidentally rubbed the lamp, a genie appeared. This genie was able to give Aladdin whatever he wanted, including a palace and the sultan's daughter as his bride.

In 1898 the founders of this small settlement, located in the extreme northeastern corner of Wyoming, felt they couldn't do much better than to name their fledgling community Aladdin, in the hope that this name would bring them good luck and riches.

Fame, if not fortune, did arrive. In September 1906, President Theodore Roosevelt established the nation's first National Monument just west of Aladdin. There the rocky pillar of Devil's Tower thrusts skyward 865 feet from the ground.

Recently, two lucky--and plucky--young residents have brought widespread fame to the community. In 1988 and 1989, Aladdin's Marvin Garrett won the National Bareback Riding championship at the annual National Finals Rodeo show held in Las Vegas, Nevada. And his younger brother, Mark, twice won the National

High School Rodeo Bareback Championship.

The settlement's thirteen residents have the good luck to find mail and groceries handy in Aladdin's century-old general store. The landmark doubles as the community's contract post office.

But the genie bringing riches must still be waiting for just the right touch on the lamp to wake him from his twentieth-century nap.

AMIGO, WEST VIRGINIA

The congeniality of people in New Mexico provided inspiration for the name of this small community in southern West Virginia.

When one of the town's early settlers visited New Mexico on a vacation, he was struck by everyone's friendliness. What really impressed him was the frequent use of the word *amigo*, Spanish for "friend."

Upon his return home, he not only renamed his coal mine the Amigo Coal Company, but he also applied the name to his other businesses in the area. Finally, he capped his efforts by naming the town Amigo. This all took place in the early 1900s, the era of the "company town," when a dominant industry often built and controlled a town.

Today Amigo, surrounded by handsome mountains not far from the city of Beckley, has a population of approximately four hundred very friendly people.

AROMAS, CALIFORNIA

Lying in a coastal valley in the California foothills just nine miles east of Monterey Bay, this small community came by its name honestly.

Early settlers immediately discovered that a sulfur spring at this location emitted a pungent smell that couldn't be ignored. In 1894, when the time came for a name, the town was dubbed Aromas. Because *aroma* generally means "a pleasant, often spicy odor," it took a nimble imagination to wind up with "Aromas" to describe this sulfur smell!

Oak-covered hillsides protect this warm, sunny valley from high winds, and the climate is moderated by the Pacific Ocean. A population of 850 now enjoys an occasional whiff of fresh air--from the ocean.

BAD AXE, MICHIGAN

An act of littering inspired the name chosen for this small community in eastern Michigan near the tip of the peninsula called "Michigan's Thumb."

In late April 1861 George Willis Pack and Rudolph Papst left Sand Beach on the shores of Lake Huron to lay out a state road to the town of Bay City, at the base of Saginaw Bay. Pack was the commissioner of that state road, and Papst acted as the surveyor.

Carrying their equipment with them, the two would travel until they found a likely campsite, then stop for four or five days. They used this time to explore the surrounding area, get the lay of the land, and select the best location for the road. It was their custom not only to mark their stopping-places on the plat map, but also to name each of these campsites.

Arriving at their third camping spot, located about halfway between Saginaw Bay and Lake Huron, they set about getting organized. While surveyor Papst was out gathering firewood, he discovered an old campground that contained relics of past campers. He picked up a worn-out axe with a broken handle. The blade was all but gone and was so chipped away that its cutting edge had been reduced to a jagged point.

"I've found an axe, but it's an awfully bad axe," Papst said when he returned to camp and showed his find to his companion. Hearing this, Commissioner Pack proposed that they name this campsite Bad Axe. Papst agreed and wrote the name in their survey record.

The two men suspected that the axe had belonged to a great early-day hunter, George Martin. Before breaking camp to move on, Papst lettered "Bad Ax" onto a small basswood slab and dovetailed the wood into a notched tree.

When Papst and Pack returned to Sand Beach several weeks later, a leading merchant asked them where Bad Axe was. Some hunters had been out in the area and stumbled onto the sign. Papst, with tongue in cheek, told the merchant that it was a new town he and Pack had founded.

Another sign, in the form of a plaque, has recently been placed in Bad Axe. It commemorates the last campaign stop of President Richard M. Nixon, who appeared here before twenty-five thousand people on April 10, 1974, to lend support to a Republican candidate. The candidate later lost his special congressional election.

Bad Axe may be the only American community whose name not only was inspired by a litterbug, but also was chosen long before there was even a community to name!

BALLPLAY, ALABAMA

If nations could settle their differences the same way the early inhabitants of the area now known as Ballplay did, we can only imagine all the resources that could be diverted from armaments into a better life for the peoples of the world.

Before we look at Ballplay's technique, let us first examine a few methods used elsewhere to settle disputes during the same decade. In 1790-1791, for instance, Congress authorized a force of fifteen hundred troops to clear out and destroy the Indian settlements along the Scioto and Wabash rivers in Indiana because these Indians were waging war on the white settlers. About the same time, a Frenchman, Edmund C. Genet, arrived in the U.S. and began to outfit ships to raid the commercial vessels of England, Spain, and Holland for France. He also tried to incite U.S. citizens to march on what are now South Carolina, Georgia, and Florida, which were all under the flag of Spain at that time.

In 1794 Congress was threatening war against Great Britain over the duties charged on the tonnage of vessels arriving on our shores. In western Pennsylvania that same year, discontent with the law levying duties on distilled spirits led to an open insurrection by the populace, and the rebellion spread to the state of Virginia. President Washington issued a proclamation against the insurgents, to no avail. He finally had to call out the militia to quiet them down.

Problems with France broke out in 1797. A treaty between the U.S. and Great Britain was disturbing the French, who were suffering through their own bloody internal revolution. French ships proceeded to capture vessels flying the American flag. These hard feelings continued into the following year, with the U.S. retaliating by capturing French ships.

But what does all this have to do with the naming of Ballplay, a community located in northeastern Alabama quite near the Talladega National Forest and beautiful meandering Weiss Lake?

In the late 1790s the Cherokee Nation, led by Little Turkey, and the Creek Nation, headed by Menewah, found themselves in a disagreement over the line that determined the dividing point between their two territories. They decided to settle their squabble in a manner acceptable to both sides.

The two chieftains agreed to have their braves play a ballgame similar to lacrosse, and used this means to settle their dispute. Later on, the spot where the game was played became known as Ballplay.

That ballgame system seems like a good idea. Perhaps the time has come for a new kind of "League of Nations."

BATH, INDIANA

The United States boasts several communities named Bath, including one in New Hampshire and another in New York. These Baths, founded in the latter half of the eighteenth century, were named after the city of Bath, England. But the hamlet of Bath, Indiana, came by its name in a different way.

This Bath was founded in 1830 near natural mineral springs. Promoters soon built a hotel and advertised their mineral baths as a cure for all human ills.

Now modern medicine offers a variety of treatments for our ailments. No one has traveled to Bath, Indiana, to take the healing waters for many years. The old hotel has disappeared along with the ambitious peddlers of curative baths.

But Bath remains, its springs still offering mineral water to the sixty-five residents who delight in this particular Bath.

BIMBLE, KENTUCKY

This southeastern Kentucky town with a population of eight hundred claims the unusual distinction of being named for a team of oxen.

A story passed down for generations explains that in 1898, when the settlers were deciding on a name, an early resident was tilling his farm with the assistance of a pair of oxen. He called one ox Bim, and the other Bill.

Folks just looked out into the field and found their new town's name, the euphonious contraction of Bimble.

BLESSING, TEXAS

In 1904 it came time to seek a post office for an area twelve miles north of Matagorda Bay on the Gulf of Mexico, about halfway between Houston and Corpus Christi.

Mr. J. L. Pierce, a local cattle rancher, wanted the

name of the new town and post office to show his appreciation for the Southern Pacific Railroad laying tracks near his spread, the "Rancho Grande." Prior to that, he'd had to drive his livestock some forty miles to the nearest railroad for shipment.

The name Blessing was not Pierce's first choice. However, when he petitioned the postal authorities to name the town "Thank God," the authorities in Washington rejected that name. Pierce settled for Blessing.

Three years later Pierce erected the Blessing Hotel. It is still in operation, graced with state and national historical markers. The hotel's restaurant has gained acclaim for its fine food, including a write-up in *Southern Living* magazine.

Today, approximately one thousand people reside in Blessing, Texas.

BOULEVARD, CALIFORNIA

It was a highfalutin name for a combined country store, stage stop, and post office along a country road near Interstate 8, just north of the Mexican border. Mrs.

Ruby, whose husband was appointed Boulevard's first postmaster in 1909, always claimed credit for the name.

Her inspiration came the day that Barney Oldfield and his entourage stopped at the store to refresh themselves. Oldfield was a famous early race-car driver who had set a sixty-mile-per-hour speed record in 1903, and his arrival created quite a sensation in the hills thereabout.

Word spread quickly through the neighboring area. Suddenly the quiet road was lined with horses, wagons, and cars, all bringing spectators to gaze at the celebrity. Mrs. Ruby emerged from the store, took one look at the crowd, and exclaimed, "It looks just like a boulevard!"

Barney Oldfield whizzed off shortly thereafter and in 1910 reached a new milestone of 131.724 miles per hour, more than double his earlier record. He was one of 110 original inductees into the Automobile Racing Hall of Fame in 1952.

The Boulevard postmark now represents home to nearly thirteen hundred residents, most of them traveling as fast as Barney Oldfield did when their town became a Boulevard.

BROTHERS, OREGON, and SISTERS, OREGON

These Brothers and Sisters grew up in central Oregon.

Sisters came first, in 1870. The pioneers who settled at the edge of both the Willamette and the Deschutes national forests named their community for three nearby mountain peaks, known as Faith, Hope, and Charity.

Thirty years later, a family with six stalwart sons homesteaded not far away. Naturally, their small settlement became known as Brothers.

These days we find Sisters growing faster than Brothers. Some eight hundred people have Sisters' zip code and only forty-five have Brothers'.

BUSY, KENTUCKY

In 1929 the citizens of this southeastern Kentucky community, after much thought, submitted several carefully chosen names for their newly approved post office.

The post office department claimed its employees were too busy to check if any of the submitted names were already in use in Kentucky.

They made the point permanent by simply calling the town Busy.

CAPTAIN COOK, HAWAII

Vacationers who wing to Hawaii for a winter holiday in the sun are probably unaware that they follow in the footsteps of an important eighteenth-century Pacific explorer and British navigator, Captain James Cook.

After joining the British navy as a seaman, Captain Cook progressed quickly to positions of command. Beginning in 1768, he made extensive voyages from

England to explore the Pacific.

In 1776 Cook sailed from England on his third and final voyage to the Far East. After rounding the Cape of Good Hope at the southern tip of Africa, he reached New Zealand.

Cook then charted his course to the northeast, and in January 1778 he came upon a chain of twenty islands extending across a stretch of more than sixteen hundred miles of Pacific Ocean. The Captain promptly named his discovery the Sandwich Islands, to honor the Fourth Earl of Sandwich, the first lord of the British admiralty.

Hoisting his sails again, Cook pressed on to the west coast of North America. A skilled navigator, this intrepid explorer mapped accurate charts of his journey, which took him as far north as the Bering Strait west of Alaska.

As cold weather approached, memories of those balmy Sandwich Islands beckoned to the Captain and his crew. They returned to harbor for the winter on the west coast of the largest of the islands, later named the Islands of Hawaii.

The natives were so impressed by Captain Cook that their priests proclaimed him a god in January of 1779.

The story lacks a happy ending, however; there are risks as well as rewards in the explorer business. Within a month of his deification, the captain was slain by islanders in a dispute over a stolen boat!

While the Earl of Sandwich has left his name to us only at lunchtime, Captain Cook's name has lived on in the area where he anchored his weary crew for a winter's respite. These days there are two thousand Captain Cook residents where the sailor sojourned and perished. Their town is one of the few communities on the map of the islands to bear an English-language name.

CASHTOWN, PENNSYLVANIA

We can only wonder whether any early settlers of this community traveled the eight miles on November 19, 1863, to hear President Abraham Lincoln give his famous Gettysburg Address. Located on U.S. Route 30 in the beautiful Appalachian Mountains just eleven miles north of the Maryland state line, this community of approximately three hundred remains a quiet place to live.

Cashtown apparently received its name from the business practices of an early tavern keeper or store owner. After a few unhappy situations resulted from extending credit, the merchant's business sense dictated that he demand cash for all goods and services. In an era when farmers depended on credit to get them to the next harvest, it was unusual for a merchant to insist on no credit, just cash. Area residents started referring to the settlement as Cashtown.

On August 8, 1833, a post office was established for the community and the name Cashtown became official.

No doubt these days even Cashtown's merchants will accept your travelers checks, MasterCard, or Visa.

CLIMAX, MINNESOTA

"For want of a nail, the shoe was lost," goes the old saying. In this town's case, the adage could have been, "Except for a chew, the name would have been lost."

While moving into their new home, a member of the locally prominent Steenerson family kicked up a plug of Climax Chewing Tobacco from the ground. Seeking a name for the fledgling settlement, he decided that Climax would be a good name for their community.

Climax was founded in 1896 and today boasts a population of approximately 250 people. It is located along U.S. Route 75, not far from the Red River, which separates Minnesota and North Dakota. About fifty miles north is the Fargo, North Dakota, and Moorhead, Minnesota, area.

To the south and east lie most of the ten thousand lakes that Minnesota legend tells us were made when the hoofprints of Babe, Paul Bunyan's blue ox, were filled in with melting snow.

COWPENS, SOUTH CAROLINA

The Battle of Cowpens, considered a turning point in the struggle against Great Britain, was waged north of this colonial settlement on January 17, 1781. Here, Brigadier General Daniel Morgan and one thousand colonials turned back British troops under Cornwallis and preserved the Carolinas from England's control. Cornwallis eventually surrendered his forces at Yorktown, Virginia, some nine months later in the final American victory of the Revolutionary War.

At an earlier time, the community was known as Hampton, a more elegant name. After a treaty was signed removing the local Cherokee inhabitants, white settlers began to graze their cattle on the natural grasslands and to build pens to hold their livestock. The hard work of a farmer named Hannah achieved fame when opposing armies clashed on his land. This crucial Revolutionary battle was fought on and around the site where Hannah had constructed his cowpens. The encounter was recorded in America's history as "The Battle of Cowpens." The residents of Hampton soon changed their town's name to reflect the Revolutionary victory nearby.

The community remained small until after another war, the War Between the States. In 1873, during postwar railroad building, the Airline Railroad laid its track through Cowpens on its route between Charlotte, North Carolina, and Atlanta, Georgia.

In June of each year, the twenty-two hundred residents of quaint Cowpens host a celebration, "The Mighty Moo Festival." Veterans of the World War II aircraft carrier "Cowpens," nicknamed "The Mighty Moo," gather for a spirited annual reunion, which does not limit its toasts to milk.

CYCLONE, PENNSYLVANIA

There by the grace of nature, and postal rules, went Simpson.

If Cyclone had been located twelve miles farther north, it would have been in the state of New York. Instead, it lies in northwestern Pennsylvania, very close to the eastern edge of the Allegheny National Forest where the Allegheny River courses through the area.

The village started as Simpson. But in 1885, when the townspeople of Simpson applied for a post office of their own, the request was approved on the condition that the name be changed, because the Commonwealth of Pennsylvania already had a Simpson.

The residents substituted a really rare town name, Cyclone, inspired by a nearby area where a twister had struck. Today, oil and lumber industries support this community of 650.

And where else can we find two churches, two service stations, an elementary school, and a volunteer fire department, all in the center of a Cyclone?

DAMES QUARTER, MARYLAND

The enclave of 1700s settlers had been taking a particularly hard battering from the guns of pirate ships as they tried to protect their settlement near the tip of a narrow peninsula. Fortunately, they were located in a spot that was somewhat sheltered against the marauding attacks from the sea, and they withstood the onslaught.

The pirates, frustrated by their inability to prevail over the area, began referring to the location as "The Damn Quarter." Nothing they did seemed to help them gain access to the land. They were never successful in any attempt to subdue the colonists.

In time, more pious heads interfered with the name by which their community had become known. Apparently, they didn't want to change its designation too much, they just wanted to be rid of that one unseemly word. Slowly, the town began to be called the more acceptable Dames Quarter.

Today Dames Quarter, whose post office was officially established in 1856, boasts a population of 150. In that same year, the Republican party was formed and Abraham Lincoln emerged as a national figure. Just nine years later, this area, along with southern Virginia, was filled with searchers looking for Lincoln's assassin, John Wilkes Booth.

Living beside beautiful Chesapeake Bay at the southern end of Maryland's Eastern Shore, the majority of townspeople have continued to occupy themselves with the oyster-and-crab-fishing industry of the region.

Other than a few modern conveniences, not much but the name has changed since those early pirate days in Dames Quarter.

DEATH VALLEY, CALIFORNIA

Few spots in this world have the contrasts of temperature and altitude that this section of east-central California claims. Located just to the west of the community of Death Valley is the Death Valley National Monument. This park, which is visited by hundreds of thousands every year, has within it the lowest point in the Western Hemisphere at Bad Water, 282 feet below sea level, and, twenty-four miles to the west, Telescope Peak, topping out at 11,049 feet. Ninety miles to the northwest is Mount Whitney, California's tallest mountain, with an altitude of 14,495 feet.

The temperatures on top of the local mountains dip below zero degrees Fahrenheit--and that doesn't take into consideration the wind chill factor! Contrast these temperatures with those of Death Valley! The hottest temperature ever recorded in the United States was 134 degrees Fahrenheit on July 10, 1913, at Death Valley. Heat reaching 125 degrees is common during the summer months. And rainfall is scarce, with an average for this area of less than 1.5 inches per year.

A favorite tourist attraction is a cluster of Spanish-style buildings known as Scotty's Castle, located at the northern edge of the park. These structures were built between 1922 and 1933 by Walter E. Scott, known as "Death Valley Scotty," a colorful resident who lived there for thirty years.

But how did Death Valley acquire its name? In 1849 the unrelenting sun and incredible heat battered a frightened band of would-be gold miners lost in this fearsome desert. The party's dreams of striking it rich in California's gold fields to the north had been replaced by despair over the slim prospect of getting across the forbidding terrain alive. They named the area Death Valley, and Death Valley it remains today. While a stroll across this below-sea-level desert in the noonday summer sunshine is not recommended, nevertheless reality has not been as harsh as the name suggests. Back in 1849 only one of those lost miners perished.

Borax deposits were discovered in the area in the early 1870s, and mining of borax began in the early 1880s. The twenty-mule team that hauled the ore out became famous. Gold, copper, lead, and silver were also discovered and mined. Mining towns with such interesting names as Bullfrog, Greenwater, and Skidoo sprang up only to become ghost towns when the ore ran out.

In 1933 this unusual valley was made a National Monument. The four hundred present-day residents along with visiting tourists and campers have their own U.S. post office to postmark Death Valley on correspondence mailed to more prosaic destinations.

DEFIANCE, IOWA

The 350 citizens now living quietly in this western Iowa community still chuckle over the tales of their more obstreperous ancestors.

The years from 1850 to 1854 saw the first three buildings erected--a harness shop, an implement store, and a post office. A stagecoach stop was established to service travelers going to or arriving from Harlan to the south and Dunlap to the west. Called Willow Creek, the community seemed to be on its way.

But the railroad surveyors came along and unsettled this tranquility. They disclosed plans to lay tracks one mile to the east. Townspeople objected, and wanted the tracks put closer to their settlement.

Despite fervent protests from the townsfolk, the railroad officials stood their ground. They announced that they would move the commercial buildings of the town to a new site near a large pond close to the new tracks. The railroad authorities even had a name ready for this new town--Marmon.

This really set the people off. They objected to being located near the pond. The railroad crew came and drained the pond for them. The community still was not happy. Folks began calling themselves Defiers, and their town Defiance.

But the railroad prevailed. The tracks were laid where the railroad wanted them, the buildings were moved where the railroad wanted them, and a large "Marmon" sign was erected near the tracks by a railroad representative.

The people, moved against their will, remained unhappy with this turn of events and continued vociferously with their grumbling and complaints.

It wasn't long before another railroad representative arrived. He hopped off the train and replaced the "Marmon" sign with one reading "Defiance."

The railroad builders are no longer the enemy. But today's residents still stand together against the caprices of changing weather and economic conditions--in Defiance.

DETOUR, MARYLAND

Amid rich farmland fifty miles northwest of Baltimore and seventy miles north of Washington, D.C., the town of Detour boasts a population of approximately one hundred.

Two centuries ago, Detour got its start as Double Pipe Creek, named after a nearby creek. The settlement was founded in the 1790s by Joshua Delaplane. He purchased six hundred acres, then built a dam and set up a grist mill, a woolen mill, and a sawmill.

Francis Scott Key, the author of the "Star-Spangled Banner," was born two miles outside of Double Pipe Creek. And nine miles to the west is the community of Thurmont, where Camp David, the presidential retreat, is located.

But in 1905 the Western Railroad, after laying its track through the area, insisted that the folks change their town name.

"Double Pipe Creek is just too long for our form," the officials complained. Residents would have to shorten the name--or the railroad would do it for them.

A leading citizen, Daniel P. Saylor, called a town meeting to choose a new name. Saylor had done some traveling in the Midwest, where he had seen many signs with the word "DETOUR." He liked the word, so he proposed it as the new name for the community.

Some insist that neither Saylor nor his fellow citizens knew what the word meant. Nevertheless, a majority cast their votes for Detour, and that has been the name ever since.

Today, when road work is taking place in the area, temporary signs often proclaim a startling, "Detour to Detour."

DEVILS ELBOW, MISSOURI

Devils Elbow shines brightly in the rich treasure of colorful town names in this region of south-central Missouri. Other settlements in and around this section of the Mark Twain National Forest include High Gate, Buckhorn, Competition, Plato, Success, Bucyrus, and Licking. All are within forty miles of Devils Elbow.

By the 1850s the railroad builders were laying new tracks across southern Missouri in their push westward. Their insatiable appetite for wooden rail ties literally was the downfall of the virgin forests along the way.

Hungry to own their own land, squatters in the area were working hard to fell the trees with hand tools and then to saw them into railroad ties. The railroads paid them with land deeds.

But first, thousands of ties had to be floated downstream on the Big Piney River, steered by long pike poles in the hands of brave workers balancing on the "rafts" of floating ties. All went well until they reached a bluff where the Big Piney curved sharply. Invariably the ties failed to make the sudden turn and piled up in logjam after logjam.

Breaking apart the jams and getting the rafts of ties moving again added time, effort, danger, and difficulty to the lumberjacks' work on the river. They called the dreaded spot "A devil of an elbow."

Today's 420 residents of Devils Elbow enjoy a peaceful scene--devoid of railroad ties, but vivid with memories.

DRYTOWN, CALIFORNIA

Along historic State Route 49, a meandering road named for the 1849 California gold rush, travelers come upon the towns of Pilot, Angels Camp, Chinese Camp, Nipinnawasee, and Drytown. Also close to Route 49 are the communities of Rough and Ready, Mormons Bar, and Coarsegold. And nearby is the site of James Wilson Marshall's 1848 gold discovery at Sutter's Mill, which triggered the California gold rush.

In the hectic year following Marshall's discovery, San Francisco grew from a small town to a bustling city of twenty-five thousand, while outfitting hordes of would-be gold miners passing through on their way to the mountains. By 1850 so many people had arrived in California that it was admitted to the Union.

This gold rush settlement sprang up in 1848, and a total of twenty-six saloons quickly opened to accommodate thirsty prospectors. In jest, the rough and tumble miners began to call the community Drytown, and the name stuck.

One of Daniel Boone's offspring followed the lure of gold, and a Boone granddaughter was born in this community just west of the Sierra Nevada mountain range.

EMBARRASS, WISCONSIN

Early French Canadian and American influences resulted in the naming of a small community located in northeastern Wisconsin.

Embarrass is located thirty-five miles west of Green Bay and ten miles southwest of Shawano. A large Menominee Indian Reservation is less than twenty miles to the north, and beautiful Lake Winnebago lies thirty-five miles to the south.

Lumbering was the livelihood of the first white settlers here. When French Canadian lumberjacks attempted to float their logs down the nearby river to the sawmills, they found the water shallow. Worse yet, the logs repeatedly got hung up on rocks, protruding tree roots, and other debris.

In frustration, the loggers named the waterway the "Riviere Embarrass." *Embarrass* is the French word meaning "to obstruct, to entangle, or to impede." When the English-speaking settlers arrived, they Anglicized the name to Embarrass River. The community took its name from the river when it became incorporated on June 8, 1895.

The present population of this agricultural town is 575. It is remarkable that such a small community supports a bank, a hardware store, three garages, a grocery store, three bars, one church, a wool carding mill, a beauty shop, a furniture factory, and a 125-bed nursing home with twelve units of apartments for elderly residents.

FIDDLETOWN, CALIFORNIA

"All work and no play" was not the motto of this California gold rush town east of Sacramento. The miners were serious about panning for gold. But when the flow of water slowed to a trickle in the dry season, their placer mining came to a frustrating, though temporary, halt.

As they waited . . . and waited . . . and waited for Mother Nature to cooperate, did the gold miners grumble and gamble? Of course. Did they idle away the hours drinking and playing poker? Well, perhaps.

But several of these miners had music in their bones as well as gold fever. Some had brought their fiddles along on the long trip west. They kept each other's spirits from sagging by playing their fiddles, with a bit of song and dance to pass the days and nights.

With all those fiddle players in the camp, the community was dubbed Fiddletown--and it has been Fiddletown ever since those 49ers fiddled away their spare time.

FREEDOM, MAINE

Does the word *plantation* conjure up visions of the antebellum South? The community we presently know as Freedom, Maine, was settled in 1794 as Smithton Plantation, *Massachusetts!* Not Maine, but a state that is located two states to the south!

Town founder Stephen Smith was a fourth-generation American and had fought under George Washington during the American Revolution. Smith was later to become grandfather to the famous Smith brothers of cough drop fame.

By 1813, during the War of 1812, the "Plantation" was incorporated as a town under a new and patriotic name, Freedom.

The year 1820 brought another milestone when, as a result of the Missouri Compromise, the state of Maine was carved out of the State of Massachusetts and attained statehood as a "free" state.

Freedom lies approximately twenty-five miles from the Atlantic coast in east-central Maine. The state capital, Augusta, is thirty miles to the southwest; Bangor is the same distance to the northeast.

In its heyday, around 1850, Freedom was home to close to one thousand residents. Today, about five hundred townspeople can proudly say they live in Freedom.

FREEDOM, WYOMING

The founders of this small community, which straddles the line separating Wyoming and Idaho, found the freedom they desired amid natural beauty. The present-day population of 450 is virtually surrounded by the massive Caribou and Targhee national forests. Hoback Peak, topping off at 10,864 feet, is twenty-four miles to the east. Grand Teton National Park lies fifty miles to the north, and Yellowstone National Park is less than one hundred miles in the same direction.

Freedom, with one side of its main street in Wyoming and the other in Idaho, was founded near the end of the nineteenth century. Today's residents have the choice of paying long distance rates to phone their friends across the street, or else walking a few steps to see them in person.

But how did Freedom get its name? After polygamy was forbidden in 1890 by a manifesto of the Church of Jesus Christ of Latter Day Saints, and the Utah Territory followed suit, some Mormons balked at giving up their lifestyle. Men with more than one wife at a time now came in conflict with the laws of Utah and the rest of the United States.

The first settlers in Freedom were Mormons who fled Utah and together figured out how to outsmart the authorities. They proceeded to build homes for their polygamous families, placing one wife and her children in Wyoming, and a second in Idaho.

When the local sheriff appeared on the scene to arrest a bigamist in either Wyoming or in Idaho, his quarry hightailed it over to the other state across the street--out of legal reach--and thus to freedom.

FRIENDSHIP, TENNESSEE

Back in 1878 there were two country stores about a mile apart. One was in the valley and the other was on the top of a hill.

When government officials came along to set up the first post office in this western Tennessee settlement, they met with the two proprietors. Naturally, each store owner wanted the new post office located in his store.

Finally the two storekeepers agreed to compromise and have the postal facility established halfway up the hill, halfway between their stores. Then came a handshake "for friendship's sake."

That's when the postal department representatives suggested calling the place Friendship. Ever since it was made official in 1913, the townsfolk have lived together in Friendship.

This community of approximately 750 has seen its business district develop around the post office site. The local Bank of Friendship depicts that famous handshake on its checks.

GAS, KANSAS

It was Gas, Kan. from 1893 until the post office killjoys spoiled the fun and changed all state abbreviations to two letters. Now the town is simply called Gas, KS.

But there's a solemn lesson for our wasteful society in the boom and bust history of this southeastern Kansas community.

On a chilly December day in 1893, the drillers exploring for natural gas were running out of coal to run their rigs. Suddenly they struck gas. It was a fine strike-- four million cubic feet a day of natural gas.

As the word spread, other companies moved in to sink their gas wells on thousands of acres in the area. In 1907 gas production peaked at a billion cubic feet daily, an apparently inexhaustible supply.

Men flocked in to work the gas fields, and numerous

smelters and manufacturers moved their operations to the source of cheap fuel at Gas. In the first decade of the twentieth century, one local company alone employed twenty-three hundred workers and produced 40 percent of the world's zinc.

Confidence was unbounded. Two miles from Gas, the county seat boasted the largest courthouse square in the country, two blocks long in each direction. Around the circumference ran a perforated pipe. When they opened the jets each night and lit a match, a dramatic wall of flame surrounded the courthouse square.

Civic pride indeed preceded the fall. Suddenly, pressure in the wells began to drop, and production of the "inexhaustible" supply of natural gas plummeted. Between 1908 and 1910 the town ran out of gas. Most of the new industries had to close their gates. The workers moved on; even their houses were hauled out of town.

Nearly eighty years later, vegetation is just beginning to grow again on the wasteland scarred so long ago by the first sulfuric acid plant built west of the Mississippi River.

Today's five hundred residents of Gas, Kansas, and the equal number living just beyond the city limits, are wiser and more frugal in their use of natural resources than were their forebears at the turn of the century. And none of them makes a living from local natural gas.

GEORGE, WASHINGTON

George Washington was past his youth when the American people followed his vision and established a new, idealistic nation. And likewise, Charlie Brown was past the half-century mark when he followed his vision and created the brand new desert town of George, Washington, in an irrigation district ten miles from the life-giving Columbia River in central Washington.

Unlike his indecisive little namesake in the "Peanuts" comic strip, this Charlie Brown was a pharmacist who turned his considerable energies from his chain of retail stores to a prescription for a wholesome new community.

First he bought 339 desert acres from the U.S. Bureau of Reclamation. Next he enlisted the aid of a University of Washington city planning professor to lay out a dream town, complete with lights, water system, and city streets named for varieties of cherries.

George, Washington, was dedicated on July 4, 1957. For the first time, the United States had a town and post office with the name of George, Washington. No other town would be able to make that claim.

The celebration that took place featured a half-ton cherry pie baked in a brick oven specially constructed for the occasion. A number of dignitaries were present, including Albert Rosellini, the state's governor.

Charlie and his equally energetic wife, Edith, erected Martha's Inn (named, of course, for George's wife), to serve visiting tourists and truckers as well as the burgeoning local population. The Browns seeded the community with additional retail businesses, later selling them off to others who moved into town.

Four years later, three hundred residents followed Charlie's vision and incorporated their city. There were builders and workers from nearby dams on the Columbia River, as well as residents of nearby communities, all hoping that life would be a bowl of cherries in George, Washington.

And indeed, the town celebrates its continued growth with an annual Washington's Birthday Cake, along with that huge Fourth of July cherry pie each year.

We would like to think that the benevolent spirits of the community's two forebears, George and Charlie, hover approvingly just out of sight.

HARMONY, CALIFORNIA

The early history of Harmony, California, was penned by an anonymous historian, who then pinned it to the post office wall.

This very small community, with a population of only eighteen, is perched along the Pacific Coast on picturesque State Route 1 about halfway between the late publisher William Randolph Hearst's castle, San Simeon, to the north, and San Luis Obispo to the south.

The town grew up around a creamery back in 1869.

44

The dairy farmers of the area were a fractious lot, with feuds and bitter rivalries a standard way of life. But after one fatal shooting, a successful truce was called. The farmers pledged to live in harmony thereafter, and so they did.

There have been a few noteworthy days since in what has become a community of working artists, according to retired postmaster David G. Sprague and current postmaster Tom Rousseve. In the 1920s and 1930s it was William Randolph Hearst's custom to entertain screen stars at lavish parties at San Simeon. On one such occasion, Sprague reported, "The silent film heart-throb star of the 1920s, Rudolph Valentino, stopped by to use (the) toilet on the way to the castle."

Things calmed down in Harmony until June 1990, when the owner of the 2.25-acre unincorporated community put the entire town up for sale. The asking price was $1.8 million, and the offer received wide media attention. Even the Cable News Network (CNN) ran the story, and an inquiry was received from as far away as Germany. But the town hasn't sold, and Harmony still prevails.

HELL, MICHIGAN

Among theologians there may be differences of opinion as to the exact location, if not the existence, of Hell, but there is no argument among the residents of a small hamlet approximately fifty miles west of Detroit.

Back in 1842 George Reeves purchased a mill in the area now known as Hell. He installed a large dam (pardon the expression) and added a grist mill, followed by a distillery and a stagecoach stop. He now had the beginnings of a village.

A few years later, local farmers began showing up in the still unnamed locale, ready to spend their leisure time by having a bit of fun. They found they could raise Mr. Reeves's hackles with their harassment and soon began asking him what he planned to call his little village, which by this time included several homes, a school, and a race track.

Becoming more and more annoyed at their incessant questions, Reeves, with some temper, answered them and, in the process, named the town.

"You can call it Hell for all I care!"

And Hell it was, flourishing from 1846 until it nearly died out around the year 1890. The grist mill burned in 1872, and the other businesses and buildings slowly disappeared. Only a family farm remained.

The locale came to life again in 1929 when new settlers arrived, bought the mill pond, and rebuilt the dam. Soon they were selling lots for cottages to entice others to settle. They named the nearby lake Hi-Land Lake and gave the town the same name.

But old habits are hard to break. Some of the new arrivals began using the name Hell and they even organized a successful petition drive to get it on the Michigan state map.

Enter Mel Reinhart. A promoter with an eye for the

macabre, he opened a novelty shop called the "Den of Iniquity" in the early 1960s. He hired young men to dress as the devil and even had them tour far and wide with floats advertising his various enterprises. He became mayor of the village and head of the Chamber of Commerce of Hell. He officiated at over fifty marriages in Hell in one year, and acquired a U.S. Weather Bureau station for the community. A city park was established and called Hell's Half Acre.

Reinhart really hit his peak when he organized "Satan's Holiday" and attracted over ten thousand visitors one year. It is said that the streets were so full of people that late-arriving sightseers could not get out of their cars!

With Reinhart's death, the growth of the town almost stopped. The novelty shop was closed for a time, but has now been reopened. Interest has waned in recent years. But the lake is still called Hi-Land, and the town is still called Hell.

Hell now has an annual Buzzard's Festival in May or June, with an arts and crafts show, square dance, and occasionally a traveling circus. Hell's post office opened on April Fool's Day, 1990, to serve two hundred Hellions and an additional four hundred people living nearby.

The United States Weather Bureau recently closed down the local weather station that for years provided television weather reporters across the nation with official temperature readings from Hell on scorching summer afternoons.

HOME, KANSAS

"There's No Place Like Home" to more than 150 citizens of this small community in northeastern Kansas, a dozen miles south of the Nebraska state line. A large sign posted for travelers arriving from the east proclaims just that--"There's No Place Like Home."

Although unincorporated, Home, Kansas, was settled more than a century ago by pioneers from eastern states and abroad. When the community was granted a post office in 1874, the townspeople chose the name of Dexter. The postal authorities stepped in and squashed that, because Kansas already had a town called Dexter.

The citizens assembled again to pick an alternative name. Since the post office was located in a settler's home, the group decided on the name Home.

In 1884, just a month after the cornerstone of the Statue of Liberty was laid, G. W. Van Camp officially platted the townsite and changed the name to Home City. But, as usual, change didn't come easy; Home is the name that has stuck through the years.

Around the turn of the century, Home was an active, prosperous community serviced by the St. Joseph and Grand Island Railroad. However, in 1905 a disastrous fire consumed the city, and it never fully recovered.

Home is proud of John Riggins, a star of the National Football League during the 1970s and 1980s, who grew up just twenty miles outside town.

Apparently everybody came back home for a festive centennial celebration on September 15, 1984. The count of celebrants was ten times Home's population, all enjoying a parade of one hundred units covering the length of the main street in town.

To the visiting relatives and friends at that day's centennial events, "There's No Place like Home" brought a special joy and nostalgia.

HOOT OWL, OKLAHOMA

The great majority of travelers using the Will Rogers Turnpike, which bisects northeastern Oklahoma from Tulsa to the junction where the states of Oklahoma, Kansas, and Missouri meet, are not aware of the very small hamlet of Hoot Owl that is less than twenty miles to the east. But if the travelers are also sports enthusiasts, they may find a look into the area worthwhile. Within a short drive are the Salina, Snowdale, Spavinaw, and Cherokee recreational areas. Just a few miles to the north is the Grand Lake of the Cherokees, and to the east is the Kenwood Indian Reservation. For those who like the big city life, Tulsa is within an hour's drive to the southwest.

There was some anguish when the time came to name the settlement in March 1977. Different names were proposed and just as quickly discarded. It was finally decided, due to the large number of owls inhabiting the hollow that embraces the community, to adopt the name of Hoot Owl.

If you decide to relocate to Hoot Owl, there should be plenty of room. The present population is four. And it has its very own city hall!

HOPE, NEW JERSEY

To tell the story of the grand experiment of Hope, New Jersey, one has to begin with the city of Bethlehem, Pennsylvania, which lies thirty miles to the southwest.

In 1735 members of a protestant group, the Moravian Sect, emigrated to the United States from Moravia and Bohemia to escape religious persecution. They founded the town of Bethlehem in 1741. As the town grew, the Moravians sent missionaries up the Delaware River to seek converts.

On these journeys, the missionaries passed through land owned by Samuel Green Jr., and often spent the night. Becoming interested in the church's teachings, Mr. Green wanted to start a community like Bethlehem on his land. He offered one thousand acres to the Moravians to establish such a settlement. The Moravians did not want to accept the land without paying for it, so they purchased the acreage for one thousand pounds sterling.

The first Moravians arrived on the land in 1769. Not until five years later, when the land was surveyed, the town plan drawn, and additional settlers in residence, was there an established community. This was one of the first planned communities in the United States, dating back to before the Revolutionary War.

Legend has it that in 1775 the townspeople deposited appropriate church-related names into a hat in order to select a name for their new town. Hope was pulled out and that became the name. This was particularly fitting, because the new townspeople were quite hopeful for the future of their budding town.

For nearly twenty years the town flourished under Moravian leadership. But the community started to decline in the early 1790s, and by the turn of the century the population had dropped below one hundred. It was then decided by the Moravian Church in Europe to abandon their experimental community. The church members were sent to other Moravian towns and the land was sold in 1807 to several Pennsylvanians.

The last Moravian service was conducted on Easter Sunday, April 17, 1808. The town of Hope had lasted just thirty-three short years under the Moravian Church's leadership.

Today the town preserves nearly two dozen structures from those earlier days. Houses, log cabins, a grist mill, a log tavern, churches, and a long house (some dating as far back as 1769) can be seen on a walking tour.

Hope is located just south of Interstate 80 in beautiful northwestern New Jersey, less than ten miles east of the Delaware River, which separates Pennsylvania and New Jersey.

HORSEHEADS, NEW YORK

Pioneer children of the early 1800s found great pleasure in jumping from one bleached horse's skull to another in this area a few miles north of Elmira, New York. Their fun was to cease in 1830 when the bones disappeared with the construction of the Chemung Canal.

But where did the severed horse heads come from? And why would there be close to forty skulls lined up in a row?

The "Legend of Horseheads" tells us of the five thousand soldiers, led by Revolutionary War General John Sullivan, who set out in 1779 from Easton, Pennsylvania, to confront and defeat the powerful forces of the Six Nation Iroquois Confederacy. The American troops hoped to cut off the supplies to the British by destroying the villages and crops.

The Indians and Tories fled north after the Battle of Newtown in late August, with General Sullivan and his troops in hot pursuit.

The heavy rainy season had done its work in a large hemlock swamp that was located near where Horseheads stands today. Some of the cattle and pack horses became mired in the resultant mud and had to be destroyed.

When Sullivan's troops returned in late September, many more horses became exhausted and died. Others, not fit to travel, were killed. All told, more than forty horses were dead.

Another story states that when their supplies failed to catch up with them, Sullivan's troops, fearing starvation, were forced to butcher and eat the steeds, leaving the heads where they lay. The Indians, upon finding the remains, arranged the skulls in a line on the trail and referred to the area as "The Valley of Horses' Heads."

The community, on Route 14 just north of Elmira, was first incorporated as Fairport (or Fair Port) in 1837. The town reverted to Horse Heads in 1845, and changed again forty years later to North Elmira.

The townspeople objected so strongly to this latest change that in 1886 the name of the town was once again changed, this time to the one-word form of Horseheads. Today Horseheads boasts a population of approximately eighty-three hundred.

INK, ARKANSAS

This small community lies in western Arkansas only twenty miles from the Oklahoma state line. The lovely

Quachita Mountains surround the town. Pencil Bluff, Umpire, Hon, Blue Ball, and Jenny Lind are neighboring communities.

Gathering to select an official name for their community at the time of incorporation, the townspeople met together and listened intently to their leader reading the instructions.

"It says here," he drawled, as he passed out the ballot slips, ". . . to 'please write in ink.' "

And they did.

IXONIA, WISCONSIN

A population willing to take a chance named this Wisconsin community.

In 1846 the town of Union, just thirty miles west of Milwaukee, was being divided in two. Folks living in the portion lying in township 7 had already made up their minds to call their community Concord. However, the residents of the area within township 8 to the north were having much difficulty coming to a decision, and their future name remained in limbo.

Finally, in desperation, the assembled citizens agreed to deposit slips of paper containing all the letters of the alphabet into a box and have letters selected until they could make a word out of them.

Mary Piper, a child living in the community, was chosen to do the honors. Slowly, she pulled out letters, including I, X, O, N, I, and A, and Ixonia became the name from that day forward. Residents believe they have the only community in the United States with that name.

John Lewis, the smallest midget in the world at the time, was born in 1857 in Ixonia. He stood only two feet, three inches, and weighed nineteen pounds during his adult years. He was more than a foot shorter than the celebrated Tom Thumb. Lewis was the oldest of seven children in his family, and the only one of short stature. He died in 1881 at the age of twenty-four, and is buried in Ixonia.

Serenely beautiful Holy Hill is close by to the northeast. This Catholic shrine was established in 1906 by the order of Discalced Carmelite nuns, which had been organized in the late sixteenth century. A beautiful panoramic view from atop the hill awaits visitors. To the north is another scenic point, Sinissippi Lake. Aztalan State Park is less than fifteen miles to the southwest.

Where Winnebago and Pottowatomi Indian tribes once roamed, Ixonia today has a thriving population of three thousand.

JACKPOT, NEVADA

It must have been confusing to the traveler stopping in at Cactus Pete's Casino to drop a few quarters into a slot machine that afternoon in 1982.

The gaming action had all but ceased, and a funeral service was in progress! Roy Spence, until recently the kitchen supervisor at the casino, had died, and his eulogies were being offered just thirty feet from his former work station. Alongside Roy in the casket were his favorite fishing rod and reel.

Such is the flavor of this community located on the Columbia Plateau in northeastern Nevada, smack up against the Idaho border. Route 93, which bisects the community, is the longest highway on the North American continent, stretching from Fairbanks, Alaska, to Guatemala in Central America.

Jackpot sits on deep lava bedrock. Streams and rivers have cut deep canyons, leaving steep ridges. Game fish in the rivers and deer and antelope in the hills offer outdoor enthusiasts a veritable recreational heaven.

Jackpot's elevation is exactly one mile. In most of Nevada an average of two people populate one square mile. Jackpot has one thousand residents, mainly supported by casinos and cattle-ranching. The largest open-pit copper mine in the world decorates the town of Ruth to the south, while to the southwest lies the Geyser

Basin, pulsating with active geysers and bubbling mud.

Until 1954 the residents of Jackpot had been receiving their mail on a rural route out of Contact, fifteen miles to the south. Three times they had petitioned the federal postal authorities for their own local post office. Three suggested names had been rejected.

Finally, inspired by the cascade of coins dropping out of a slot machine into the hands of a lucky player, the townspeople submitted the name Jackpot. The U.S. postal authorities agreed, and the world had its first post office housed in a gambling casino!

Street names carry out the theme of the town's biggest industry. In a north-south direction run Keno, Roulette, and Slot. East-west streets are Pinochle, Poker, Ace, Casino, Twenty-one, and Dice. Several other streets are named after casino operators.

Several events enliven Jackpot throughout the year. This community considers itself the Cross-Country Air Racing Capital of America and holds approximately fifteen airplane races each year. The annual Western States Hollering contest is also held near Jackpot. And for years a man (or could it have been a leprechaun?) showed up every St. Patrick's Day to play the slot machines garbed in a green suit, green shirt, green tie, and green shoes, with a green shamrock pinned to his lapel.

When you think about it, that traveler dropping in on a funeral in a casino wasn't encountering anything too unusual--for Jackpot, Nevada, that is.

JET, OKLAHOMA

On September 16, 1893, six Jett brothers, along with thousands of other land-hungry homesteading settlers, rode into the Oklahoma Territory to stake their claims on the newly opened land. These brothers, Twigg, Warner, Newt, John, Dick, and Joe Jett, staked out their allotted acreage in the Cherokee Strip in north-central Oklahoma, twenty-four miles south of the Kansas state line.

They soon petitioned the postal authorities in Washington, D.C., to give their new town a post office with the name of Jett. Something got scrambled in the red tape of the government mechanism, and the last "t" was dropped from the name. The community became known as Jet.

A solitary oak tree, brought along by Twigg Jett in his wagon, still lives, its branches offering shady comfort to the Jett descendants living on the original homestead. Twigg had lovingly planted the tree and requested his family not to let anyone do harm to it. At ninety-five years old, the oak stands tall and proud.

The town currently has a population of about 350. And at least one grand old oak tree.

JOT 'EM DOWN, TEXAS

There is variety in Texas. One can travel just a short distance and leave a city with the sophisticated name of Paris and be in one with the totally down-to-earth name of Jot 'Em Down. Both are in the northeastern corner of

Texas and are less than eighty miles northeast of Dallas. Nearby are communities with the interesting names of Novice, Telephone, Direct, and Ben Franklin. The city of Denison, birthplace of Dwight D. Eisenhower, and the Eisenhower State Park are a short distance to the northwest.

Back in the late 1920s or early 1930s, when radio played the role television does today in American households, this tiny hamlet needed a name.

One of the nation's favorite radio shows was "Lum and Abner." Many a family across the country would gather around the radio so as not to miss a word of the show, most of which took place in the show's general store, called the Jot 'Em Down store. The townspeople adopted the store's name for their town.

Jot 'Em Down has a population of all of fifteen today, making it somewhat smaller than its more worldly neighbor, Paris, to the northeast. And Dallas, of course, is a bit larger yet.

KING AND QUEEN COURT HOUSE, VIRGINIA

A five-word name for one small town? That's King and Queen Court House, Virginia. A strange name it is, in a country that prides itself on its democratic traditions and in which many cities and towns, at the Post Office Department's urging, have deliberately sought out short names.

But there's a heap of American history embodied in those five puzzling words.

In 1691, eighty-five years before our country broke away from the British crown, King William and Queen Mary were the monarchs of England. Virginia was one of their colonies in the New World.

58

During that year, English colonists settling near Chesapeake Bay founded King and Queen County, named to honor their sovereigns. They followed the local colonial custom of calling their county seat, where they erected their court house, by the county name followed by "Court House." A few other U.S. communities retain Court House in their names to this day.

William and Mary have been gone for centuries, and we emerged from the rule of kings and queens more than two hundred years ago. Still, the nostalgic anachronism lingers, when the citizens of this quiet village mail their letters postmarked "King and Queen C.H., Virginia."

KNOCKEMSTIFF, OHIO

The village of Knockemstiff lies serenely in the hilly terrain of southern Ohio, not far from U.S. Route 50 and only a dozen miles from Chillicothe.

White settlers came to this part of Ohio from Virginia when the new territory beckoned to them after the American Revolution. Their descendants were a rugged lot with a well-deserved reputation for rough language and frequent fights. But the settlement was not actually named until 1881, when country preacher Nathan Eveland's neighbors asked him to suggest a name.

"The most appropriate name you could give this place is Knock 'Em Stiff!" he answered with some rancor, remembering the numerous fistfights he had witnessed in the community. And the name has stuck for over a century.

This was Indian country before the Revolutionary War. Mingo and Shawnee warriors dug the colors for their war paint from the clay banks of the nearby Paint River and buried their fallen chiefs here as well.

The heritage left by a still earlier Indian civilization, the Mound Builders, is much in evidence in this area. Thousands of Indian mounds in various shapes--round, square, four- and eight-sided figures, and animal shapes --are in evidence. These earthen structures were used by a long-since vanished Native American culture in religious rites and burial practices. Archaeological excavations have uncovered artifacts from a complex extinct Indian society unknown by most Americans. Just thirty miles southwest of Knockemstiff is one of the more surprising mounds in Ohio, the Great Serpent Mound, shaped like a giant serpent with open jaws. The jaws alone measure seventy-five feet, and the mound's total length is 1,348 feet, including a tail formed into a triple coil.

Ten miles west of Knockemstiff lies the Seip Mound, which has been excavated. The Mound City Group National Monument is less than fifteen miles to the northeast.

The name Knockemstiff has had its troubles. Periodically a newcomer to town suggests changing the name to something more "acceptable." So far these attempts have failed, and Knockemstiff remains, a quiet community in the beautiful hills of Ohio near two other hamlets, Yellowbud and Lick Skillet.

LETTER GAP, WEST VIRGINIA

Once upon a time, so they say, before women wore jodhpurs or blue jeans for riding, even before they graduated from riding side-saddle, the following incident took place at the time a settlement was seeking a name.

A sassy young woman came riding through this town in the northwestern part of West Virginia.

One young man wasn't too busy to watch her progress down the main street mounted on her big horse. Impressed, he hailed her with an important observation.

"Hey, lady. Your skirt has a gap in it!"

She looked down at her skirt, then turned and looked the man square in the eye.

"Let 'er gap," she replied. She rode off, and the town had a name.

Perhaps she was hurrying to visit a neighboring

community, such as Burnt House, Pickle Street, Exchange, Millstone, or Gassaway.

LOCO, TEXAS

How would you like to live in a town named after a weed? Not only a weed, but a weed that is not necessarily pretty? At least, the *effects* of the weed aren't pretty.

Loco, Texas, is located just south of the Prairie Dog Town Fork of the Red River at the point where the Texas Panhandle begins to spread east to encompass the greater portion of that vast state. The city of Childress is close by, as is the state line of Oklahoma. The lovely city of Amarillo is one hundred miles to the northwest.

The loco weed was found in abundance in this area by the early settlers. When the weed was eaten by the cattle, they would become "crazy" and then sick.

In 1930, when the community desired a post office, the weed's name was submitted, and the postal authorities agreed to the selection. *Loco*, the Spanish word for "crazy," became the town's name.

LULU, FLORIDA

Lulu is a small town to which the expression "Don't

blink or you'll miss it" really does apply.

You'll pass through Lulu on State Road 100 just south of the Osceola National Forest, halfway between the communities of Lake City and Lake Butler. Lulu is a mere thirty miles southwest of the outskirts of the sprawling city of Jacksonville. All that is visible from the highway is the combination general store and post office, a roadside tavern, and one house. The rest of Lulu's population of approximately 150 are out of sight on graded dirt streets nearby.

Once upon a time, Lulu was a thriving community with seven stores, two barbershops, a doctor's office, and a railroad stop. Then the boll weevil reared its ugly head and destroyed the crops, and the town shrank.

But how did Lulu acquire its name? When first settled after the Civil War, the town was called Hagen. There was another town in nearby Alachua County known as Hague Station. This caused confusion, and so the townsfolk of Hagen were requested by the postal authorities to select another name.

One of the old timers passes on the story that in 1888 Walter Gillen, an influential citizen of the area, named the community Lulu after his girlfriend.

Lulu soon left town without marrying her suitor, leaving only her first name behind.

MAGNET, NEBRASKA

Don't let the population figure of seventy fool you into thinking this Magnet hasn't had any pull.

B. E. Smith came to this area of northeastern Nebraska and began a settlement he called Magnet, hoping the name would draw residents. Through the years the town attracted numerous businesses, including two grain elevators and even an opera house.

But the community has also attracted a series of fires and two tornadoes. The second twister swept through on May 6, 1975, and leveled just about every garage in town. Each time the town rebuilt. In 1976 Magnet pulled in an honorary title as a Bicentennial City.

MARATHON, FLORIDA

This community in the Florida Keys actually started out as Key Vaca. It is located midway between the mainland of Florida and Key West.

In the early years of this century, Henry Flagler, one of the major early developers of the east coast of Florida, was building the Overseas Extension of the Florida East Coast Railroad. His company used Key Vaca as a location for construction supplies and material, and as a food supply depot to feed the thousands of construction workers employed in the enterprise.

The story is told that when the line had nearly reached Key Vaca, a remark was made that it had become an endurance contest--a marathon--to reach that point. Key Vaca has been known as Marathon ever since.

While the railroad to Key West was under construction, two kinds of boats made regular visits to the area. One type, the "liquor boats," enjoyed a brisk trade with many of the workers. The others, sent by Key West churches and referred to as "gospel boats," sought to meet the spiritual needs of the railroad builders.

Today, Marathon is but one of many beautiful spots on the trip through the Keys. These days travelers and residents drive on a modern post-World War II highway and bridge system. Mr. Flagler's east coast railroad was abandoned after the yearly hurricanes had taken their toll. A roadway was installed, but the first road built from the mainland through the Keys was too narrow for the cars and trucks of today and a newer, wider highway has replaced it.

Only the ruins of the old bridges rising from the water, seen from the new highway, remind us of the marathon efforts of those long-ago construction crews.

MARYS IGLOO, ALASKA

Before recorded time, the first Americans crossed

over the Bering Strait from Asia to reach the North American continent. It was in the western portion of Seward's Peninsula in western Alaska, close to the Bering Strait, that Mary built her igloo more than one hundred years ago. The truth is, it was a sod house, not an igloo.

When the white settlers and miners arrived, beginning in 1886, they named the place Marys Igloo, after the sturdy Eskimo woman who lived there. Mary lived to be more than one hundred, and her village has grown to four hundred residents, many of Eskimo heritage. Those with young families move away to the nearby town of Teller so their children can attend school.

Whenever there's time, they return to Marys Igloo to fish and hunt, and most plan to retire back home. Some of them still remember Mary, though she's been gone more than thirty years.

They understand, too, why she chose to build her home and live out her days in that far northwest spot known as Marys Igloo.

MIDNIGHT, MISSISSIPPI

One night in the late 1800s, a high-stakes poker game led to calamity for one unlucky plantation owner and to a name for this Mississippi town.

After a series of bad hands, the unfortunate gambler

put up most of his cotton plantation--and lost once again. The winner promptly ended the game by rising and pulling out his pocket watch.

"Well, boys. It's midnight," he announced, "and that's what I'm going to call the land I just won. Let's quit."

The area has been called Midnight ever since. Named officially in 1897, the town has the distinction of being both a poker pot and a settlement located over an extinct volcano.

Life has changed in Mississippi since plantation days. The farmers surrounding this agricultural community now put part of their acreage into soybeans, wheat, oats, and catfish ponds. But they still raise cotton around Midnight, bringing the crop to the community's three cotton gins after the harvest.

As for the poker games, there is no word about what the stakes are nowadays.

MUCK CITY, ALABAMA

This unincorporated rural community took root before Alabama became a state.

In 1818 Lawrence County was formed, with the city of Moulton named the county seat. The same year the area that would become Muck City was settled several miles west of Moulton on State Highway 24. Alabama joined the union the next year.

Today, the one hundred inhabitants of this quiet little hamlet are served by one store, one church building, and one church school building. Some twenty houses dot the area.

Approximately four miles to the west is the Old Town Creek Baptist Church, founded in 1818. Another six miles to the west, Highway 24 crosses the route of the Byler Road, the first state road in Alabama. Byler Road connects Tuscaloosa on the south and the banks of the Tennessee River on the north, a distance of some 120 miles.

How did this fine community lying in the north-western corner of Alabama acquire such an interesting name? It seems that it rained often while the first road in the settlement was being built out of the black soil with hand labor and mule-drawn wagons. The mixing of the soil and rain produced such a muck that it hampered the road work, with both workers and mules becoming mired down. The settlers began calling their community Muck City, and the name stuck.

NALCREST, FLORIDA

Have you ever wondered what happens to letter carriers when they retire? Did you think they just walk away into the sunset? Ride off in their little Jeeps?

The answer just might be discovered in the central Florida community of Nalcrest, located several miles east of Lake Wales and a bit northeast of Frostproof.

In 1963 the National Association of Letter Carriers established a retirement community for its members and their spouses and named it Nalcrest--that's NALC-rest.

A bronze statue with an interesting history greets visitors in the town square. No confederate soldier or general on horseback holds the place of honor in Nalcrest. This statue is a likeness of a different sort of hero, a somewhat portly mailman named Richard F. Quinn, complete with a letter pouch and a handful of letters ready for delivery.

Quinn was an organizer of the NALC and was its first president during 1881-1895. He was chosen to have his likeness immortalized in bronze. The statue stood watchfully in front of the main Philadelphia post office for more than twenty-five years.

When a new downtown post office was built in Philadelphia, the statue disappeared. It was finally located in 1942 by William C. Doherty, then president of the letter carriers' union. After much searching, he discovered it packed in a crate in the attic of the new post office.

The statue was uncrated and housed in the NALC office building in Philadelphia until 1963. Upon the founding of Nalcrest, it was again crated and shipped to the fledgling town, unpacked once again and raised to the place of honor it has today in the center of this very special community. No letter carriers deliver the mail here. All the residents pick up their envelopes at the post office in the town square.

NEEDMORE, PENNSYLVANIA

The family members were hard at work constructing a shed, when a nosy and officious neighbor appeared on the scene. After due observation, this self-appointed advisor announced the obvious.

"You need more lumber."

Local lore tells us the citizens decided then and there to dub their growing settlement Needmore.

Other towns in various states have had the same name bestowed upon them, indicating they were in need of something more. In Kentucky alone there are at least five Needmores.

One thing the five hundred citizens of Needmore, Pennsylvania, don't need more of is magnificent scenery. The town is located in south-central Pennsylvania, in the middle of the Appalachian Mountains, only eight miles north of the Maryland state line.

NOCATEE, FLORIDA

Nocatee evolved from the Florida Seminole Indian word *Nakiti*. The Seminoles left this verbal legacy when they retreated into the Everglade swamps to escape being exiled to Oklahoma. It means "What is it?" or "Where is it?"

To answer the questions, it is a community of nine hundred residents located six miles south of Arcadia in southern Florida's DeSoto County.

Any other questions?

OIL CITY, PENNSYLVANIA

This community of thirteen thousand, lying in the northwestern corner of the Commonwealth of Pennsylvania, came by its name in a bluntly honest manner.

O. C. Chambers writes, "The village [is] at the mouth of Oil Creek. The air reeks with oil. The mud is oily. The rocks hugged by the narrow street perspire oil. The water shines with the rainbow hues of oil. Oil boats, loaded with oil, move through the oily stream, and oily men with oily hands fasten oily ropes around oily snubbing posts. Oily derricks stand among the houses.

. . . [I] think the above explains [the city's name]." It couldn't have been said better!

Edwin L. Drake fostered the oil industry on a large scale in 1859 with his famous well in this area. Oil City was founded in 1871 and boasts the oldest producing oil well in the world.

When Oil City was founded, the country's population, according to the census bureau, was 38.5 million, and total federal expenses were just under $300 million dollars. In 1871 a delegation of prominent ladies approached the Judiciary Committee of the House of Representatives, claiming the right to vote on the basis of the Fourteenth and Fifteenth Amendments to the U.S. Constitution. Eventually, women did get the right to vote, with the ratification of the Nineteenth Amendment in 1920.

Much has changed since the early days of Oil City, but oil is now much more important to the lives of Americans, especially the residents of oily, oily Oil City.

OIL CITY, WISCONSIN

The fifteen residents of this small hamlet in southwestern Wisconsin lead a more sedate life today than did some of their ancestors.

The first settler, Esau Johnson, arrived at the upper end of the Kickapoo River valley in 1842, six years before Wisconsin was admitted to the Union as our country's thirtieth state.

In the mid-1860s, after the community had grown to a population of several hundred, a smooth-talking stranger named Tichnor wandered into the area and convinced the locals that he was an oil expert. He suggested that the topography of the region looked promising for oil.

He spent his time conspicuously going about the area looking the land over for signs of oil. It wasn't long before he did indeed spot "liquid gold" in the form of an oil slick on a pond.

Tichnor quickly formed the Gem Petroleum Company, with himself as the head and largest stockholder. He signed leases with the area farmers for oil exploration on much of their land at high prices and long leases.

"Oil fever" began to run high, as people came from the surrounding area to see and taste. All agreed oil was there, and most wanted to invest.

The company's stock was in great demand. Tichnor, who held the great majority of the stock, finally "reluctantly" agreed to sell most of his stock to a number of anxious buyers and new friends. Numerous wells were sunk in an attempt to find more of the precious fluid, but all that was pumped from the earth was water.

Soon someone discovered that Tichnor, the oil expert, had sunk a barrel of oil under a spring--the source of the oil slick. By this time, the fly-by-night developer was long gone. With the investors' money, of course. Some of the local citizens were badly hurt financially.

The "oil expert's" visit had two other long-lasting results.

Some of the purest, most healthful water in America was discovered, and Oil City, Wisconsin, had a name it would never have had if oil hadn't been "found."

OLD GLORY, TEXAS

This patriotic-sounding community in north-central Texas actually started out as Brandenburg in 1908. But with the entry of the United States into World War I in 1917, anti-German feelings ran high throughout our land. Residents of this little village with the same name as a major city in Germany were acutely aware of the animosity toward all things German.

At a meeting held to discuss the situation, it was decided to rename the town. Different names were proposed, but the chosen one was as American as apple pie. What better way to show where the townsfolks' loyalties lay than to embrace the name of Old Glory for their town?

And Old Glory it has been since 1917. This community, with a population of seventy, is located approximately fifty miles northwest of Abilene and Fort Phantom Hill. Lake Stamford lies twenty miles to the east.

ORIENT, MAINE

Back when the 1700s became the 1800s, the settlers in this area of Maine were well aware that they were located at the very eastern edge of their state and, they assumed, the eastern edge of the United States. At the time, it was the fashion to give communities classical or exotic names. Thus inspired, the residents selected Orient--meaning east--as their community's name.

In actuality, there is a goodly hunk of Maine which extends farther east than Orient, and today there are other American communities located east of Orient.

Furthermore, Orienteers are two miles west of the international border with the neighboring Canadian province of New Brunswick.

In any case, everything is relative. East is east--almost.

PARACHUTE, COLORADO

A creative surveyor named this area back in 1879. To the rest of the Hayden survey party he pointed out the ridges and gullies traced by drainage patterns down the steep slopes of the Roan Plateau, comparing the effect to the tightened lines of a descending parachute. Three years later the first white settlers made their home at Parachute Creek.

The parachute was no modern twentieth-century invention by folks who wanted to bail out of airplanes. Leonardo da Vinci sketched it first nearly five hundred years ago, but he was too busy to try out his concept.

The first man who leapt with a parachute and lived to brag about it was a French scientist who jumped from a tower more than two hundred years ago. His chute worked, so it's only fitting that the word *parachute* is of French origin and means "preventing a fall."

You'll find Colorado's Parachute along Interstate 70 as it stretches alongside the Colorado River in western Colorado. It's taken more than one hundred years for Parachute to billow up from the pioneer Hurlburt family of 1882 into a population of 350 Parachuters today.

Thanks to land speculators who renamed it Grand Valley, the town lost its airy moniker for about seventy-five years. The promoters were trying to snare travelers looking for the Grand River valley near Grand Junction, farther west. The Colorado River, flowing by Parachute, was first called the Grand River.

Since the town retrieved its original name in 1980, western Colorado has again wisely packed its own Parachute.

PARADE, SOUTH DAKOTA

A careless postal employee's goof resulted in this community in central South Dakota marching on as Parade.

Located on the Cheyenne River Indian Reservation, which joins the Standing Rock Indian Reservation to form a massive tract of land extending into North Dakota, Parade lies thirty-five miles west of the Missouri River. The most productive gold mine in America is located at Lead, 120 miles to the southwest in the beautiful Black Hills. And just one hundred miles due west is the exact geographic center of the fifty United States.

South Dakota was home to the famous Hunkpapa Teton Sioux Indian, Sitting Bull, who ended his days on the Standing Rock Reservation. He had been the leading medicine man in preparing the tribes for the battle of the Little Big Horn in the neighboring Montana Territory. In this July 25, 1876, battle, known as "Custer's Last Stand," U.S. Army General George Custer and all his troops lost their lives at the hands of Indians led by the great Oglala Sioux Chief, Crazy Horse.

Now--the goof. In 1920 the name Paradee, honoring the man who had donated the townsite, was submitted to the U.S. Post Office Department for approval. When the paperwork had finished making the rounds in

Washington, D.C., it arrived back with the final "e" omitted. The townspeople felt it just wasn't worth the hassle and red tape to straighten out the mistake, and they've been Paraders ever since.

Parade is near the communities of Glad Valley and Faith. Norm Van Brocklin, famous football quarterback and coach and the youngest of ten children, was born at home in Parade.

It was easy to get up a scrimmage then, but today Parade has a population of only two--but it has its own post office.

PARADOX, COLORADO

The first uranium ore was discovered at the Raja mine on Carpenter Ridge northeast of the community of Paradox. A sample of this strange ore was sent all the way from Colorado to famous chemist Marie Curie in France to be analyzed.

Paradox is now a ranching community of around two hundred. The first settlers had arrived during the late 1870s and had a post office approved in 1882. The first general store was not built until 1885.

The community lies in western Colorado, close to the Utah border and is named for Paradox Valley where the settlement is located. This valley perplexed the surveying party that first measured its twenty-three-mile length and five-mile width. Contrary to the usual behavior of streams, the Dolores River, which bisects the valley, does not run through it lengthwise, but cuts across the width of the valley. A puzzled surveyor mapped the area as Paradox Valley around 1876, and folks have been enjoying the Paradox ever since.

PEERLESS, MONTANA

Did self-confidence and civic pride culminate in the choice of Peerless when this northeastern Montana town was named around 1910?

It would indeed be understandable if today's 350 residents, living amid rolling plains eleven miles south of the Canadian border, hold their community in Montana's wheat and cattle country to be the unrivaled best home town.

But the pioneer settlers had something else entirely in their thoughts when they chose to call their settlement Peerless. They were honoring not abstract excellence but rather the brand name of the Peerless Tobacco and Peerless Beer that were shipped in large quantities into town and quickly consumed in equally large quantities.

Brand names have come and gone in eight decades, but the community inspired by one of them remains Peerless.

PICNIC, FLORIDA

Picnic is no more than a wide spot in the road at the junction of State Roads 39 and 672, the latter also known as Picnic Road. It is located some thirty-five miles due east of St. Petersburg (with Tampa Bay in between), and only twenty miles southeast of Tampa.

Before the turn of this century, Picnic was known as Hurrah, not in the "hoo-ray" sense, but from an Indian word contributed by former residents of the area. Where Hurrah Creek and the Alafia River converge, people from the surrounding area would gather for fish fries, bar-b-ques, picnics, and a good time. People would walk for miles or ride in their horse-drawn buggies to join the festivities.

Over time, the name Hurrah was used less and less, and the name Picnic prevailed. It seems those who gathered there thought of the place as a picnic.

PIE, WEST VIRGINIA

Pie can be found in westernmost West Virginia, with the Kentucky state line close by to the west and another small town, Red Jacket, just to the east.

Early in its history, the Post Office Department asked the townspeople to submit a list of possible names for their new post office and town. The name Pie was included since the community had one local resident who really loved pie--*any* kind of pie!

It seems appropriate that the small town of Crum is located just to the north.

PIE TOWN, NEW MEXICO

They stayed . . . and stayed . . . and stayed . . . .

Pie Town, at an elevation of nearly eight thousand feet, is located one-quarter mile west of the Continental Divide in western New Mexico. Mountain peaks of ninety-five hundred feet or more surround the area.

A major east-west route crossed through here in the early days. A husband and wife, heading west in their horse-drawn wagon, had just traversed the Datil Mountains and the divide when their horse died.

Rather than continue on foot, they decided to remain for a while and enjoy the magnificent views in all directions. They made a dugout to live in and filed a mining claim along a promising volcanic-made ditch a short distance to the southwest.

The woman began to make pies from dried fruit that they had brought with them. Cowboys on cattle drives soon discovered the pie-making operation, and word spread about the tasty pies and friendly welcome awaiting travelers at the settlement, by this time unofficially christened Pie Town.

When a post office was applied for, the need for a name arose. Pie Town was the only name submitted by the first postmaster in 1928, and became official when accepted.

The community periodically holds a Harvest Time Pie Festival. They were held annually in the 1930s, but things have slowed down in the hamlet. Forty citizens live in Pie Town, and a like number live outside of town.

PIGEON, WEST VIRGINIA

Early in the 1800s, the daytime skies periodically darkened over the extreme southern portion of West Virginia; no sunshine could filter through. What caused this curious phenomenon in the expanse situated just a few miles north of the Virginia-West Virginia state lines and just west of the Allegheny and Appalachian mountain ranges?

The community that is now called Pigeon was known first as Pigeon Roost, so dubbed because, until the late 1800s, millions, probably billions, of wild passenger pigeons chose eastern North America as a roosting site each year.

One early-day observer described a flock that was a mile wide that took forty-five minutes to pass a given point. Still another observer, scientist Alexander Wilson, saw a large flock in 1808 over Kentucky and believed there were 2,230,000,000 birds in the group! The great naturalist John James Audubon reported in 1813 that he watched a flock that passed in a stream that lasted for three days, blotting out the sun, with their wings sounding like thunder.

Thousands of acres were taken up with the nesting of these birds. Every tree had dozens of nests. The pigeons left little food for other creatures and traveled up to a hundred miles a day looking for food.

Pigeon hunters who arrived each year used several techniques to stalk their prey. The birds were blinded with lights and then knocked from the trees; burning sulfur was used to choke them; and trees were cut down to aid in their capture. After each of these methods, the captured birds were then shot.

The hunters ate or preserved a few of the pigeons, but most were shipped to Chicago or New York where they brought a sale price of one or two cents each.

Alas, the passenger pigeon is no more. The hunters decimated this member of the Columbidae family. The rest mysteriously disappeared. Some believe that they attempted to cross the Atlantic Ocean and became lost.

In 1914 there came a sad day at the Zoological Gardens in Cincinnati, Ohio, when the bird believed to be the last passenger pigeon in the United States died in captivity.

There are no more passenger pigeons in southern West Virginia today, but the locale's scenic beauty remains. As those who live in or have traveled this area know, the region is blessed with some of the most beautiful scenery in America.

PODUNK, MASSACHUSETTS

Yes, there really is a Podunk! It is a small community with a long history and a population of two hundred (mostly retired) residents. Located southeast of the large Quabbin Reservoir, it is part of the East Brookfield area, not far from Worcester.

Would-be humorists sometimes employ "Podunk" as a generic term to designate a rustic, out-of-the-way American small town. The genuine Podunk story might surprise them. The literal meaning of *podunk* is "a swampy place."

Until three hundred years ago, the Podunk Indians lived here amid lakes and forests. But in 1686 white settlers arrived with land grants from the English gov-

82

ernment in their hands and soon took over the Podunk territory from these Native Americans, keeping only the Indians' name intact.

Nearly eighty years passed. British colonial rule was nearing its dramatic end when a certain sturdy home was constructed in the Podunk of 1767. A full century later this house became the birthplace of the builder's great-great-grandson, Henry Plimpton, who grew up to make a unique contribution to the recreation of young people throughout much of the world.

If you've ever enjoyed roller-skating, you can thank Henry Plimpton. After graduating from the Massachusetts Institute of Technology, Plimpton invented a roller skate wheel that would bend to allow the skate to "hold the floor" at almost any angle. This invention brought about a boom in the roller skate manufacturing business, accompanied by the building of roller rinks all over the United States.

Podunk had already produced a remarkable young woman. In 1830, at the age of twenty-seven, Sarah Henshaw of Podunk ascended the pulpit of the Reform Methodist Church to become the first licensed female clergy member in the nation. This was seven years *prior* to the founding of the very first secondary school in the United States to admit women—Mount Holyoke in South Hadley, Massachusetts.

PORCUPINE, SOUTH DAKOTA

Tucked away in the southwestern corner of South Dakota, fifteen miles north of the Nebraska state line, lies the small community of Porcupine. Its neighbors are beautiful Badlands National Park twenty-five miles to the north, world famous Mount Rushmore seventy miles to the northwest in the Black Hills National Forest, and infamous Wounded Knee, Porcupine's closest neighbor, seven miles to the south. Wounded Knee is the site of the last major battle between the U.S. Army and the Sioux Indians under Chief Big Foot. In the attempt to disarm captured Indians here in 1890, a rifle was accidentally discharged. In the bloody battle the incident triggered, two hundred Indian men, women, and children were killed by U.S. troops. The Wounded Knee Massacre National Historical Site is a memorial to that tragic event.

Porcupine took its name from nearby Porcupine Butte. On the level top of this butte there grew a cluster of pine trees that from a distance resembled a crouching porcupine. It is thought that some early settlers coming from the eastern U.S., seeing the outline of a porcupine in the distant hills, bestowed the name on their new community.

Many animal names have found their way into place names, but the woodland-dwelling porcupine rarely gets that honor (most communities wouldn't want to be named for the slow-witted, prickly animal). However, the porcupine, found in forested areas throughout the United States, has lent its name to several geographic features, particularly in the west. In eastern states, however, geographic references to this slow-moving mammal, whose name is from the French for "spiny pig," are practically nonexistent.

POSSUM TROT, KENTUCKY

Credit for naming this community goes to Hyman Caldwell, via the local schoolhouse. As the teacher employed by the town in 1862, Caldwell christened the log schoolhouse "Possum Trot." It is not known whether he was referring to a local possum he occasionally caught sight of out the school window or to the well-worn path between the schoolhouse and the outhouses behind the school.

Today this community, known earlier as Frisky Ridge, boasts businesses selling groceries, drugs, ice, and furniture. Possum Trot also claims to have the largest tomato-growing, -packing, and -shipping business in Kentucky.

This western Kentucky community lies nearly twenty miles east of Paducah and even closer to the Illinois state line, thanks to a bend in the rambling Ohio River. Just a few miles to the south begins the beautiful Land Between the Lakes Recreation Area. Possum Trot is known to some as the gateway to nearby Kentucky Dam.

PURE AIR, MISSOURI

The afternoon was hot and steamy. The sultry air hung in the gullies like a blanket. As she brought her cows back up for milking, "Granny" Johnson was seen wiping her brow with her apron and muttering to herself.

"It's good to be back in pure air again!"

And so the story has been passed down since the late 1800s when this farming community in northwestern Missouri adopted the pleasant name Pure Air.

The church building was erected in 1905 to replace the little old Union Church. Times were hard, and the community ran into construction cost problems. Another denomination stepped in and offered to pay the last one hundred dollars--on the condition that the deed to the church building be signed over to them! It wasn't until 1954 that the community bought back the church and land.

Nearby are the communities of Cherry Box, Novelty, and Mystic. Hannibal, where Mark Twain grew up, is eighty miles to the southeast. Kirksville, the nearest big town, is eighteen miles to the northeast.

Local recreation areas include the Thousand Hills State Park, Long Branch State Park, and Long Branch Lake.

In its heyday, Pure Air supported a general store, a drug store, a church, a blacksmith shop, and a sawmill. Over the years a pool hall, a harness shop, and a dry goods store came and went. Residents once had a gas station and garage, a drive-in movie theater, a grinding mill, a trucking business, a school, and a doctor.

Before the television era, neighbors came together

for traveling medicine shows and all-day Fourth of July picnics. Later on there were outdoor square dances and then baseball games pitting the community entry, the "Hog Creeks," against neighboring towns' contenders.

But today it's a quieter place. All the businesses have closed. All that's left is the church, and Pure Air.

REFORM, ALABAMA

Today's nineteen hundred residents of Reform appear to have changed their ways since 1819, the year that Reform was named and Alabama was admitted to the union.

Three hundred years after Spanish explorer Hernando De Soto led his soldiers through what is now Pickens County in western Alabama, another rough band arrived in this area; this time they came to stay.

These early settlers had discovered great forests of rosemary pine, one of the finest lumber products known. The citizens built themselves a few shanties and a rowdy reputation. When Methodist missionary Lorenzo Dow arrived upon the scene, his valiant attempt to organize a revival meeting met with harassment from the irreverent settlers.

As Dow rode out of town after his revival meeting fizzled, one of the local toughs, unable to suppress a parting shot, called after him.

"Parson, we haven't a name for our town. Got a

suggestion?"

"Reform," retorted the angry evangelist as he galloped away. The name stuck.

Sadly, the rosemary pine has not reforested itself since its early decimation. The beautiful virgin timber is gone forever, and with it, the lumber industry that sustained the early settlers. But cotton, railroad transportation, and an intersection of state and federal highways have sustained this small city, incorporated since 1898.

Reform is now within easy commuting distance of seventeen universities, colleges, and trade schools. Concerts, lectures, and other cultural opportunities are available to Reform's citizens. In Pickens County, there are more than 130 churches serving nineteen separate denominations; seven of the churches are in Reform itself. Lorenzo Dow would have been proud.

It appears that the townspeople, harkening to the injunction of Preacher Dow, have taken their town's name to heart.

RESCUE, VIRGINIA

Rescue is one of the oldest towns in Virginia--indeed, in the United States. The community was founded in 1645 as Smith's Neck on a land grant to a man named William Smith. That same year a ship left Salem, Massachusetts, for Guinea, Africa, for a cargo of slaves. It was the first direct slave-trade between New England and Africa, an activity that would increasingly impact Virginia.

Settlers formed this community, located along the James River in southeastern Virginia, thirty-eight years after the Jamestown colony was established twenty miles upriver. Today, 325 Rescuers live in a locality steeped in American history. Colonial Williamsburg lies twenty-five miles north of Rescue. The Virginia state capital and capital of the Civil War Confederacy, Richmond, is seventy miles to the northwest. The towns of Bacons Castle and Chuckatuck are Rescue's neighbors, as is the Hog Island Game Refuge.

When the Smith's Neck residents grew numerous enough to rate a post office of their own, the first task of their postmaster, William Carter, was to pick a new name for the area.

"Well," he said, "your mail is being rescued from the mule's back," the customary mode of postal transportation of the day. The mules are history now, but the community and its post office have been Rescuing their mail ever since.

REVLOC, PENNSYLVANIA

In the 1910s two gentlemen, B. Dawson Coleman and J. H. Weaver, combined their energies to mine coal deposits in southwestern Pennsylvania. This necessitated founding a settlement for the miners who moved in to work the new coal mine.

Around 1911 the mine owners decided to name their new town after themselves. They combined the first three letters of Coleman's name with the last three letters of Weaver's, and the community was christened Colver.

That's only half the story. Four years later the two men were ready to expand their operation. Seven miles from Colver, they purchased additional land, opened another coal mine, and built a second town for their mine workers. By 1915 Colver had a sister city, Revloc--Colver spelled backwards.

It might appear on the road map that all roads lead to Revloc, located at the junction of Routes 22, 422, and 219. Actually, most of the traffic whizzes along on the bypass, and most days the six hundred residents of Revloc have their quiet community to themselves.

RIFLE, COLORADO

"It would be like finding a needle in haystack," the young aide grumbled to himself. And in the uncharted wilderness that was western Colorado in 1876, just finding a haystack would be nigh impossible, had one even existed there. But this mapmaker's assistant trudged on, rough sketch in hand, always with a wary eye out for hostile Ute Indians.

His boss had been out for several days, gathering preliminary data near the Grand Hog Back Range, which rises north of the river now known as the Colorado. With his thoughts on the final drawings he would make for the Hayden Survey party, the mapmaker had somehow left his precious rifle behind. A person couldn't chance being without a rifle in this terrain; it was the only form of protection against the wild animals and the fierce Indians who resented intruders in their hunting grounds.

So, he dispatched his assistant to retrieve his weapon, equipping him with a roughly drafted map. He carefully marked the spot by a creek where he remembered propping his rifle against a tree. That map, with "RIFLE" lettered by a sketch of a tree, inadvertently named the area and the long creek that flows through it.

Nowadays, roaming without a rifle is safe enough for the thirty-two hundred residents of the town of Rifle, which grew up where Rifle Creek empties into the Colorado River. Interstate 70 runs alongside the Colorado, trying to match the mighty river's flow.

The village of No Name lies east of Rifle, and the small community of Parachute is a bit farther west.

ROUGH AND READY, CALIFORNIA

The United States has had plenty of internal problems throughout its history, but the happenings on April 7, 1850, must have given the federal government and the new state of California additional cause for alarm.

Rough and Ready was named by Captain A. A. Townsend, who served under General "Rough and Ready" Zachary Taylor. Townsend had arrived in 1849 from Wisconsin with a gold-mining crew. He set up camp and called his crew the Rough and Ready.

The mining was so productive that Townsend journeyed to Wisconsin for more workers. Upon his return he found that so many miners had arrived that there was hardly space left for him to pitch a tent.

In addition to the stresses of their town's explosive growth, the miners of Rough and Ready were enraged at a new mining tax that the national government was demanding on all claims. The lack of law and order displayed by the townspeople added to the discomfort.

In early April 1850, the inhabitants of the town felt enough was enough. They held a meeting attended by most of the town's three thousand citizens. A motion was made suggesting that they withdraw from the union and set up a free and sovereign country of their own. The motion carried and the town became The Great Republic of Rough and Ready. The meeting adjourned with many angry threats against outsiders (including the governments of California and the United States) and promises not to retreat from this newly declared independence.

Colonel E. F. Brundage, organizer of the meeting, was elected president of the republic. A constitution not unlike that of the United States was drawn up and signed. But, alas, the revolt was short lived. When it was time for the Fourth of July celebration three months later, Old Glory was raised with some good old-time flag-waving patriotism. The thrust of the rebellion had spent itself and the whole occurrence faded into the past.

Rough and Ready, with a population today of about eight hundred, acknowledges its realliance with the United States with an all-day celebration on the last Sunday of June each year. Included is a play depicting the town's early history, highlighted by a reenactment of the secession incident.

Rough and Ready is near Route 20 just a few miles from the north end of the scenic and historic gold-miners' Route 49. Sacramento is forty miles to the southwest. Many old buildings, dating from the 1850s and 1860s, still stand in Rough and Ready for tourists to enjoy. The town's Chamber of Commerce is one of the oldest in the country.

ROUND O, SOUTH CAROLINA

A well-known Cherokee Indian's tattoo provided the name for this town in southern South Carolina.

As early as 1700, the white pioneers and traders moving into this area found it easier to deal with this man than with some of the other Native Americans. It was also easier to give him a nickname rather than pronounce his lengthy Indian moniker.

His nickname became Round O, derived from the tattoo of a purple medallion on his shoulder. The name seemed to please him and his fellow Indians--a succession of Cherokees adopted the name down through the years.

Several important Revolutionary War battles took place in this area, and much of South Carolina's history is associated with this area west of Charleston.

The Round O mail route serves approximately 450 families along a route that stretches over one hundred miles. Forty residents call the crossroads at Round O home. There's an appliance store, a milling company, and the post office with that one hundred-mile route.

SANDWICH, NEW HAMPSHIRE

He gets a lot of the blame for England's losing the Revolutionary War. Still, the Fourth Earl of Sandwich certainly had a lot of honors bestowed upon him, *before* he helped England lose the war.

The pre-Revolution Royal Governor of this area in New Hampshire named many places for his friends back in England. In 1763 he named this central New Hampshire town of Sandwich for John Montague, Earl of Sandwich, who later served as England's First Lord of the Admiralty during the war with the colonies. The Earl's performance is considered so incompetent that the British navy was almost useless during the conflict.

We can also remember the Earl every time we stop for a quick bite, because he is given credit for inadvertently inventing the sandwich. Reluctant to leave the gaming table during a game of cards, he ordered a servant to bring two slices of bread with some meat tucked inside. And, presto, the "sandwich" was created.

In 1849 the town that carried his name was flourishing and was under consideration as a likely state capital for New Hampshire. But the California gold rush drew many families out of Sandwich to seek their fortunes in the west and Concord won the honor.

Nowadays there are nine hundred residents in Sandwich during the winter, but the community doubles in size during the summer months.

The late movie star Claude Rains lived in Sandwich for several years, and Katherine Hepburn and Henry and Jane Fonda filmed "On Golden Pond" in the Sandwich area.

SKULL VALLEY, ARIZONA

Sounds ominous, doesn't it? The reality is quite different. With a forty-two-hundred-foot elevation, surrounded by seven-thousand-foot mountains, the three hundred residents of today's Skull Valley enjoy a moderate climate and enough rainfall to grow home gardens and dooryard fruit trees. This peaceful central Arizona community supports an elementary school, a general store, a gas station, a nondenominational church, and perhaps the oldest post office in Arizona, established in 1869.

And the skulls? An ominous sight did startle the first white settlers, who arrived in 1864 to find piles of bleached Indian skulls, the result of a bitter battle between Apache and Maracopa warriors. An attack by one hundred Indians on a wagon train of fifteen whites in August, 1866, added an additional thirty-five skulls.

By 1878 women and children joined the men, and a school was established. The town became a regular stage coach stop.

To protect settlers and freight haulers against continued Indian attacks, the federal government established Fort McPhearson in Skull Valley in 1883.

The year 1894 brought two major events to Skull Valley. First, a circuit-riding preacher, an intrepid Southern Methodist, arrived to begin Sunday services in the local schoolhouse. The iron horse arrived that same year on newly laid rails. Several freight trains still pass through Skull Valley daily, heading toward Phoenix one hundred miles to the southeast. With the passenger trains gone, residents currently resort to cars, trucks, and private airplanes for transportation.

Mines were active in pioneer days and operated through the depression of the 1930s. Now job-seekers must work on outlying cattle ranches or drive to Prescott, eighteen miles northeast of Skull Valley, to find employment.

Descendants of the pioneers and other retirees have made their homes in this scenic valley. Townsfolk are proud of their fellow citizen, cowboy and western artist George Phippen, a founder of the Cowboy Hall of Fame in Oklahoma City, Oklahoma. The Phippen Museum of Western Art in nearby Prescott also honors his memory.

Skull Valley shares its dramatic scenery and its sunsets with the neighboring settlements of Congress, Peoples Valley, Bagdad, and Nothing.

SLAPOUT, OKLAHOMA

The towns and settlements around Slapout are few and far between. This tiny town is situated at the east end of the Oklahoma panhandle, eight miles north of the corner where the Oklahoma and Texas panhandles join. The town of Fort Supply and the Fort Supply Reservoir are thirty miles to the east. Just four miles to the west is the Kiowa Creek. From the air, the South Canadian River weaving south of Slapout has the appearance of a snake.

In the depression days of the 1930s, the Works Projects Administration was constructing a highway through the area. The workers, in need of supplies, would go to a little store located where Slapout now stands and attempt to purchase necessities. The storekeeper, with only about thirty-five dollars worth of inventory, often did not have what was asked for. The men would retrace their steps to their camp and report that the store was "slapout" of the merchandise.

When it was time to install the highway sign identifying the area, the workers put up a sign saying Slapout instead of Nye, the town's previous name.

Slapout, sitting out there on U.S. Highway 270 away from almost everything, has a population of five.

SLEEPY EYE, MINNESOTA

In 1899 they brought the old chief home from the South Dakota reservation where, nearly forty years earlier, he had closed his eyes for the last time. The white settlers reinterred the remains of Lower Sisseton Sioux Chief Sleepy Eye near the lake he had loved so much. On his fifty-foot-high monument they carved "Always a Friend of the Whites."

Sleepy Eye had been a peacekeeper in central Minnesota throughout the middle years of the nineteenth century, signing the treaties that pushed his tribe of hunters off the rich land and confined those who stayed to narrow reservations along the Minnesota River. There the Native Americans tried to transform themselves into farmers, though the white settlers occupied the best farmland.

In 1862, two years after the old chief's death, some of the starving Sioux made a final attempt to regain their lost territory. They attacked an outpost of soldiers left to protect the white Minnesota pioneers. Cannon fire soon quelled the Indian rebellion, and, in retribution, the victors removed the last of the Dakota Sioux from Minnesota.

Ten years later the railroad builders brought to life a new town named for Sleepy Eye, the friendly chief.

The Winona and St. Peter Railroad Company, now the Chicago and Northwestern, extended their tracks westward across Minnesota. There they built a roundhouse to store and repair the locomotives. Railroad workers moved into the new town, along with other settlers brought in by rail. The community flourished, supporting five hotels, eight general stores, six blacksmiths, and a variety of other commercial ventures.

Located in the midst of a grain-producing area, the community soon began a long career as a flour-milling center. At peak production the Sleepy Eye flour mill, employing nearly 250 workers, could grind twenty-five thousand bushels of hard wheat in twenty-four hours.

Turn-of-the-century mansions still line the streets of Sleepy Eye. That era also produced St. Mary's Catholic Church, large enough to seat one thousand, with high Gothic arches, imported stained glass windows fit for a cathedral, and huge bells tolling their message across the prairie.

Today Sleepy Eye's thirty-five hundred residents work in a variety of agribusinesses. They celebrate their distinction as "the Goose Capital of the United States" each September 29th by observing the credo "If you eat goose on this special day, you will never want for money all the year 'round." This festival follows "Butter Corn Days" in late August and an annual "Great Grassroots Gathering."

SMUT EYE, ALABAMA

This very small community is located at the junction of County Roads 14 and 35 and State Route 239 in southeastern Alabama. It lies approximately fifty miles southeast of the state capital, Montgomery, and less than thirty-five miles due west of the Chattahoochee

River, which defines the state line between Alabama and Georgia.

Smut Eye does not lack for fishing opportunities: The Conecuh River is six miles to the west and the Pea River is four miles to the east.

In the early days of this settlement, pre-1850 as the story goes, the men of the area would gather at the blacksmith's shop. Here they played checkers, pitched horseshoes, and tried to top each other with their stories.

On many occasions, they also partook of some of the moonshine distilled in the area. This resulted in bouts of "hand scuffling," which sometimes led to more vigorous combat.

In some cases, the men would show up at home with blackened eyes. Whatever the origin, they always had the same explanation as to the cause--the black eyes were from the smut at the blacksmith shop!

Now, with the blacksmith shop out of business, the men have lost their excuse, probably resulting in fewer black eyes in Smut Eye.

STALWART, MICHIGAN

The townspeople of this community on the extreme eastern tip of Michigan's Upper Peninsula took their politics pretty seriously back in 1881. At that time the majority of citizens belonged to the stalwart faction of the Republican party. Their feelings ran so strong that they decided to name their town Stalwart.

Political winds come and go, but Stalwart is still an apt designation for these hardy folks who brave the gales of frigid winter in Upper Michigan.

STAR, IDAHO

It was once a rising star with a population greater than that of Boise, which is seventeen miles to the east. Today Star, Idaho, is a peaceful satellite community with five hundred residents, many of whom are employed in the nearby state capital.

Founded in 1864, twenty-six years before Idaho achieved statehood, this lively settlement along the famous Oregon Trail was the scene of many a murderous gunfight during its pioneer days.

The first settler erected his one-room cabin from poplars growing on his homestead along the Boise

River. He tanned animal hides into window coverings to protect the openings against intruders during the night. Miners and other travelers soon found the new settlement to be a convenient stopping place for food and lodging. Its location within a natural artesian water district assured them of a constant water source.

Education for their children was always a priority for American pioneers, so, shortly, it was time to build a schoolhouse for the growing population. The finishing touch on the construction was a wooden star, sawn from a leftover slab of wood and proudly nailed to the front door of the new schoolhouse. And Star was born.

Star was a point on the interurban railway connecting neighboring towns from the early 1900s until 1928, when the popularity of driving Henry Ford's Model T displaced the tedium of waiting for the train.

By 1908 the community was busy enough to publish its own newspaper, the *Star Observer*. Today the town supports an antique shop called the Star Gallery, a trailer factory, a sprinkling of other commercial establishments, and one remaining saloon.

SUNSPOT, NEW MEXICO

Sunspot, a dot on the map in south-central New Mexico, owes its existence to the sun.

The town, with its 110 residents, lies near the top of

the 9,200-foot Sacramento Mountains, four miles south of 8,114-foot Mule Peak, and somewhat farther from 12,003-foot Sierra Blanca Mountain.

Sunspot has a different population mix than the neighboring communities of High Rolls and Truth or Consequences have. Sunspot was created in 1952 to house the families from the Sacramento Peak Observatory, a research facility for study of the sun.

The founder and director of the observatory, John Evans, chose Sunspot as an appropriate designation for this unusual community, where the only residents are employees of the lab and their families. The observatory experts work with the most powerful equipment in the world for solar observation, and they know quite a bit about sunspots. John Cornett, librarian for the facility, reports that the name was changed in 1984 to the National Solar Observatory, and Ray Smartt took over as deputy director shortly thereafter.

Back in 1952 the name Sunspot generated some static. Some of the women in the community would have preferred an elegant Spanish name for their elite community. But John Evans's choice of Sunspot prevailed. It was intimately related to the work of the observatory. Besides, he was everybody's boss.

The ladies eventually saw the light.

SWEET LIPS, TENNESSEE

The town of Sweet Lips prospered in those bygone days before the Civil War. The general store sold *everything*, even wagons and buggies. Mule-power operated the cotton gin serving the local farmers. Children trudged to the log schoolhouse that doubled as the community church on Sundays. A grist mill, a blacksmith shop, a doctor's office, and a post office thrived in the teeming community.

Life was sweet in that cotton-based economy, and so was the water of a pure, cool, local spring. Local legend tells of a dusty traveler who stopped to drink there.

"Oh, that's so sweet to my lips," he marveled, wiping his mouth with the back of his hand. The folks who heard him began to call the unnamed hamlet Sweet Lips, and it has been Sweet Lips ever since.

The older folks in Sweet Lips still tell stories of how things were. There's still a Baptist church, a cemetery, and a grocery store. The small towns of Montezuma, Finger, Reagan, and Right are still nearby. And the Chickasaw State Park and Forest are still ten miles to the west.

But a lot has changed in Sweet Lips in 125 years. Some of the townspeople drive over to nearby Henderson to their factory jobs, and many of the younger ones have moved to faraway cities to work and raise their families. The cotton gin, the mules, the grist mill, the blacksmith, the doctor, the school, and the post office are nothing more than memories. But the spring water still runs cool and sweet.

TAINTSVILLE, FLORIDA

The people around Taintsville have a box seat for every blastoff from the John F. Kennedy Space Center, as they are about only forty miles away from Cape Canaveral. Many small lakes dot the area. The expansive beaches of the Atlantic Coast lure ocean-lovers. World-famous Disney World is but a short drive away.

It was a quieter era when this town gained its curious name. The two towns of Oviedo and Chuluota are about nine miles apart on Route 434, roughly twenty miles northeast of Orlando in central Florida. The location now known as Taintsville lay between these two towns. After fielding numerous inquiries from travelers as to where this unnamed area was, the patience of the townspeople of the nearby communities of Oviedo and Chuluota began to wear thin.

Finally, somewhat irritated, one recipient of the often-asked question grumbled, "If it tain't here, and it tain't there, it must be where it's at."

Such logic resulted in the naming of the small community of Taintsville.

TELEPHONE, TEXAS

When Alexander Graham Bell received his first telephone patent on March 7, 1876, he surely didn't imagine that soon a town in the extreme northeastern part of Texas would be named for his fledgling invention.

But that's exactly what happened. In the late 1870s the townspeople of this settlement needed a name for their community. Excited by the novelty of the new communication technology, residents chose the name Telephone for their town. And some 335 miles to the southwest lies the small community of Telegraph, Texas.

Telephone is located five miles south of the Oklahoma state line. Thirty miles to the west is the city of Denison, birthplace of Dwight D. Eisenhower and the site of the Eisenhower State Park. In the same area are the Lake Texoma Recreational Area and the Hagerman National Wildlife Refuge. A few miles to the southwest is the Caddo National Grassland area.

There is no evidence that folks in this unincorporated town, with about two hundred present-day residents, had even seen a telephone at the time they honored Bell's gadget.

TEN SLEEP, WYOMING

Communities are few and far between in this history-laden area of north-central Wyoming. The nearest towns of any size are Worland, twenty-six miles to the west, and Buffalo, sixty-five miles to the northeast.

In the midnineteenth century, a large Indian encampment, known to early trappers as the Old Sioux Camp, was located south of Ten Sleep on the Casper-Platte River, near the present-day town of Casper. Another large and well-known Indian camp was situated to the northwest at Bridger, Montana, on the Clarks Fork River. Halfway between was Ten Sleep.

The Indians measured distance by the number of nights, or sleeps, it took to travel a given distance. Many townspeople believe it took ten sleeps (ten days and nights) to get from either of those camps to Ten Sleep.

Older residents hotly dispute the validity of this story. Some say that there's no way that the Indians, traveling as they did with their families, could make the trip in ten days, especially considering the mountainous trails that had to be negotiated and the tribal custom of staying longer at good campsites. There are those who favor a story of a tribe waiting at this location for "ten sleeps" for others to join them. Another tale suggests a tribe on the move in wintertime caught in a snowstorm. They had to wait "ten sleeps" for the storm to let up so they could continue. Still another legend tells of a tribe stopping here to fish and fighting with another tribe that considered this their territory. Women and children hid in caves in the canyon while the men battled each other for "ten sleeps."

Today Ten Sleep has a population of nearly five hundred. Sheep and cattle are raised in the surrounding area, and Bentonite clay, an ancient volcanic ash, is mined in the area to be used for preserving food, enhancing detergents, molding sand, and in oil-well drilling, where it is used to hold the walls of the hole in place. Bentonite was named for Fort Benton, Wyoming, where it was first discovered in 1847.

The town supports a grocery store, several service stations, a hardware store, two bars, and several motels. A museum and cafe are open only in the summer. The Girl Scout National Center West, used by hundreds of campers each year, is six miles east of Ten Sleep.

The beautiful Ten Sleep Canyon drive leads tourists northeastward into the Big Horn National Forest. Along the way is the Powder River Pass, with an elevation of 9,666 feet. Other towns in the area include Emblem, Pitchfork, Sunshine, Letter, Spotted Horse, and Kaysee.

TIGHTWAD, MISSOURI

The community of Tightwad, with a citizenry numbering sixty-four, is located in west-central Missouri, ninety miles southeast of Kansas City.

Tightwad received its name years ago, it is said, when the local postman stopped at a store and purchased a watermelon. Not wanting to carry it with him, he arranged to leave it and pick it up when he finished his route. He returned to discover that the storekeeper had sold the melon to another customer for a higher price. With tongue in cheek, the letter carrier began referring to the store as Tightwad.

When the town incorporated in 1984, the name had already caught on and was selected as the town's name.

The name has proven to be an advantage to the local bank. The Tightwad Bank had deposits of $2.2 million in early 1986, an astounding amount for a bank in a town with such a small population. The bank draws not only residents of the area and nearby developments around Truman Lake, but also tourists who have passed through and business executives who have heard of the bank.

Think about it. Would you rather have your money in the care of a footloose and fancy-free banker, or a Tightwad banker?

TIN CUP, COLORADO

A combination of the curiosity and courage of an early gold miner, stampeding horses, and gold-laced gravel in a tin drinking cup culminated in the dubbing of this settlement Tin Cup.

Located in the Rockies of central Colorado, Tin Cup

lies five miles west of the Continental Divide and ten miles west of the 14,197-foot peak of Mount Princeton, one of the famous "university mountains," along with Mount Yale and Mount Harvard. Mount Elbert, at 14,433 feet (the highest point in the state), is thirty miles to the north. More beautiful surroundings for Tin Cup's two hundred residents would be hard to imagine.

In late 1860 prospector Jim Taylor, a Southerner, was searching for gold in the Rockies. He decided to investigate an area west of the Continental Divide known as Gunnison country. This was Ute Indian territory, where earlier miners had been massacred for having violated Ute soil.

Following his urge, Taylor successfully tracked some Ute Indians to find a route over the divide. He then returned to the town of Granite to recruit his three partners to join him on his hunt for gold on the far side of the divide.

They finally arrived and made camp in an area that now bears Taylor's name, the Taylor Park Reservoir. The prospectors' horses were spooked and scattered by bears, who apparently felt the same way toward intruders as did the Utes. While looking for the horses, Taylor stopped at a creek where he panned some gravel containing gold.

Taylor stashed the gold in his tin drinking cup. The men continued to find gold as they wandered in a southerly direction, still searching for their horses.

Upon finally locating the horses, Taylor turned to a nearby creek for a drink of water. The gravel in the bed of this creek contained an abundance of gold. Again he carried his find back to camp in his tin cup, and promptly named the region Tin Cup Gulch.

When the Gold Cup Lode was discovered in 1879, the community of Tin Cup boomed to exploit the gold strike. Hundreds of thousands of dollars worth of gold was shipped out of the area. Production began to drop in the early 1890s and was discontinued in 1936.

During the busiest days of Tin Cup, the population reached a high of six thousand. Saloons, hotels, and merchants invaded the area, vying for the miners' money. One grocer set up a large "burro train" and offered quick delivery of supplies to the miners. His charge was ten cents per delivery, as long as the trip didn't take more than one day!

Once known as one of the toughest little towns in Colorado, Tin Cup depends today upon seasonal visitors seeking not a gold strike but summer recreation.

TOAD HOP, INDIANA

Lying midway along the state line separating Indiana and Illinois, Toad Hop, Indiana, is less than five miles east of Illinois. Located south of The National Road, U.S. 40, and just west of West Terre Haute, the community is close to such interestingly named communities as Sandcut, Art, Hoosierville, Bogle Corner, and Saline City. The famed Wabash River is only a hop, skip, and jump to the east.

So why the name Toad Hop? If you listen to the old-timers' story that is the most commonly accepted, you hear that whenever the creek that ran through the community overflowed its banks in the spring, toads would be hopping all over the area.

A levee was built many years ago to contain the water's flow, and this stopped the annual appearance of the toad brigade. By that time, the name of Toad Hop had become deeply entrenched.

The name so fascinated cartoon writer Rex May, who creates the cartoon strip "Frank and Ernest" along with artist Bob Thaves, that he did a comic strip featuring Toad Hop. The strip was distributed by Newspaper Enterprise Association to papers throughout the country.

The town prospered in the late 1920s and into the early 1930s, when a local clay plant hired as many as one hundred people. The plant was followed in the same building by a mushroom-growing company. In the early 1940s the building burned and the town started to decline.

Since then, Toad Hop has just ambled along off the beaten path. U.S. Route 40, which used to go right through town, has been rerouted and now skirts the community. Today Toad Hop does without both the onslaught of toads every spring and the constant traffic down their main thoroughfare.

And most of the 150 residents like it that way.

TROPIC, UTAH

Someone once said, "Everything is relative." How

else can you explain the naming of *any* place in Utah, especially during the winter months, as Tropic?

But the early settlers of this community did select the name Tropic. Their reasoning was logical. The town's location, even though right in the path of some of the country's worst winter storms, was warm in comparison to other nearby communities. The surrounding terrain provided a protection from the elements not afforded to neighboring towns.

Tropic was founded in 1889 and is located along scenic Route 12 in south-central Utah. Tropic's 425 residents live at the edge of beautiful Bryce Canyon National Park, named for Ebenezer Bryce, who settled in this area in 1875.

And each summer they do enjoy several hot, somewhat tropical, days.

TURKEY SCRATCH, ARKANSAS

If someone stated that he or she lived in Turkey Scratch, you might be inclined to arch an eyebrow and mumble, "Uh huh. . . ."

But if you ever find yourself eight miles north of Marvell, Arkansas, on Route 243, you will find that Turkey Scratch does indeed exist. If you look fast enough, that is. If you still have doubts, just ask any of the twenty-five residents who call it home.

In earlier days this area was well known as a fine hunting ground with a variety of game, including bear. But wild turkeys were not in evidence. In an attempt to remedy this, several of the early-day settlers gathered up a fairly large flock of tame turkeys, brought them to the area, and turned them loose.

Time and nature took care of the area's lack of wild turkeys. Within a few years there were plenty of wild turkeys mixed in with the other game.

But why the name? It seems that turkeys tend to scratch fallen leaves aside while looking for food. Hunters, noting this, could easily find the turkeys' feeding areas, and they began calling the area Turkey Scratch.

In the early 1900s a small community developed. Several stores, a saw mill, a sorghum mill, a grist mill, and a cotton gin were built. Prosperity had come to Turkey Scratch!

But, as in most areas of our country, the rural areas began to lose out to the urban. The population began to shift, with many finding it necessary to move to the cities to earn a living.

The community of Turkey Scratch, fifty miles southwest of Memphis, Tennessee, is just seven miles east of the starting reference point used in the survey when the U.S. acquired the lands in the Louisiana Purchase. A few miles to the east of Turkey Scratch, the winding Mississippi River separates the states of Arkansas and Mississippi.

TWAIN HARTE, CALIFORNIA

The Twain Harte area was first occupied by the Mi-Wuk Indians who built their homes of bark and tree limbs along the lake. The community's oldest landmark, "The Rock," is a massive stretch of granite close to the Twain Harte Lake Dam.

With the discovery of gold in 1848, thousands of miners were drawn to the Sierra foothills. After the gold rush fizzled out, loggers and ranchers arrived to harvest the lumber and make use of the grazing lands. Then farmers planted orchards of pear and apple trees.

In 1861 the United States Congress decided to build a road from this area over Sonora Pass, connecting the fledgling business center of Sonora west of the mountains with the mining boomtown of Aurora. When the contractor hired to build the road ran out of money, private funds were found to finish the job. Travelers had to pay the tollgate keeper at this spot until the 1890s, when the county took over the road.

Although the settlement dates from 1861, real growth began in the mid-1920s, when a series of struggling developers promoted the recreational potential of the area. These real estate developers also capitalized on the fame of two early residents of this area, joining their names for the first time.

One was born in Florida, Missouri, in 1835 and was raised in nearby Hannibal. The other was born one year later and grew up in Albany, New York. Both became great American writers, both traveled extensively in Europe, and both resided and wrote in this area of tall pines and exquisite mountain lakes in the foothills of the Sierra Nevadas of eastern California.

Mark Twain, the pen name of Samuel Langhorne Clemens, is best known as a humorist and novelist. He is still considered a master of the tall tale. Bret Harte was another notable American writer. Most of his writing was about life in the mining towns of early California. Harte was the first editor of the *Overland Monthly* magazine, where he published his own works "The

Luck of Roaring Camp" and "The Outcasts of Poker Flat." Soon the *Atlantic Monthly* magazine of New York City hired Harte at a large salary. Harte left the *Atlantic* in 1878 and took a position in Germany, then worked in both Scotland and England.

It is ironic that a community would combine the two names for its town name, as Twain was reputed to have hated Harte. If true, this could be because Harte printed a poem, humorous in nature, in the *Overland Monthly* entitled "Plain Language from Truthful James." It became an overnight hit and began to be called "The Heathen Chinee," as it was anti-Chinese. Twain, a reformer with strong ideas and emotions, may have taken exception to Harte's poem. It is known that Twain fought for justice for the Chinese in California.

The first permanent school in Twain Harte opened its doors in 1928--after being moved intact from Confidence, a nearby mining community. The first water system, an open ditch waterway, predated the school and is still in operation. After World War II, the population zoomed. The quiet, lazy summer retreat was transformed into a growing city with a year-round population of several thousand.

TWO DOT, MONTANA

Two Dot is only one small dot on the Montana map, lying close to the center of the state. It is surrounded by mountain peaks called Little Belt, Castle, Big Snowy, and Crazy that stretch as high as eleven thousand feet.

In 1899, ten years after Montana was admitted to the union as our forty-first state, the old Sawbone Railroad was built through the spread of cattleman "Two Dot" Wilson, who branded his stock with two dots.

When Wilson donated land along the track for a townsite, the 250 who settled there just naturally christened their new town Two Dot, for Two Dot Wilson. The town with the off-beat name became a popular shipping point for wool and for the sheep and cattle raised in central Montana.

The town of Checkerboard is to the northwest, Sixteen is to the west, and Roundup is to the east. The headwaters of the Missouri River lie seventy miles to the southwest, and Yellowstone National Park is ninety miles due south in northwestern Wyoming.

Though Two Dot has shrunk to thirty residents, it was once known far beyond the surrounding mountains. Comedian Bob Hope mentioned Two Dot on one of his shows, and Hank Williams wrote a song about the town. Closer to home, its unusual name has made it the topic of good-natured jokes through the years.

TWO EGG, FLORIDA

How many communities with populations of fewer than thirty can equal Two Egg's fame? The town of Two Egg has been filmed by at least four television stations, featured in numerous newspapers including the military publication *Stars and Stripes*, and saluted by the popular television program "Hee Haw." Furthermore, Two Egg's guest book includes signatures from all over the world.

This community, once known as Allison, is located off the beaten path in north-central Florida within fifteen miles of both Alabama and Georgia. Most folks in the surrounding area are busy farming peanuts, soybeans, tobacco, corn, cotton, or watermelon. Other residents work at nearby state institutions. Marianna is the nearest large town.

In the early 1920s two brothers, Henry and Attaway Barnes, were often enlisted by a neighbor to run a distance of four miles to the nearest general store for various items. She would give the boys fourteen eggs-- twelve to trade for her grocery order and one for each of the two boys to spend as he liked.

The boys would make sure the storekeeper was aware that two of the eggs belonged to them and that they wanted to spend them on gingercake, thank you.

Soon the shopkeeper began calling them the "two egg boys." It wasn't long before the small settlement was being referred to as Two Egg, and the name stuck.

Who is the source for this story? Why, Mr Attaway Barnes, one of those "two egg boys."

Other stories are told as to the origin of the name Two Egg. One tale relates that two brothers started a store, and their first customer asked for two eggs, thus inspiring a name for the settlement. Another tells of a child entering the store, proffering two eggs, and informing the shopkeeper that his mother wanted one egg's worth of this and one egg's worth of that. Still another story tells of a man blessed with many children and little money who gave each offspring a chicken and allowed the children to "spend" the eggs their hen produced.

But, having talked with one of the "two egg boys," it is easy to reject all other stories as apocryphal.

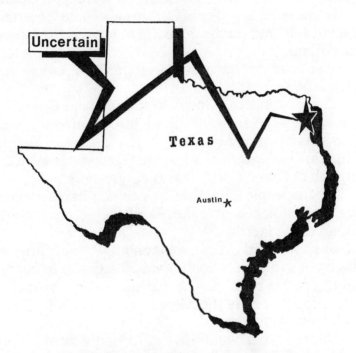

UNCERTAIN, TEXAS

One thing is certain about Uncertain, Texas. Its residents are proud of their community. All 175 of 'em! There's nothing uncertain about that!

First came Caddo Lake, one of the oldest lakes in Texas. It was formed when an earthquake blocked the Red River in northeastern Texas close to the Louisiana state line. Fish thrived in Caddo Lake. When the white settlers discovered this bounty, tent settlements on the banks evolved from fishing camps into today's Uncertain near what is now Caddo Lake State Park.

The Uncertain Town Hall occupies one-half of a

trailer, and, of course, there is an Uncertain Volunteer Fire Department and an Uncertain two-member Police Department. The community has its Uncertain Tourist Bureau and its own annual Uncertain Floating Christmas Parade. At the edge of Caddo Lake is the Uncertain Yacht Club, and on the outskirts of town is the Uncertain dump.

Two roads intersect at Uncertain: This-A-Way and That-A-Way.

The only church in town, the Caddo Lake Church of Love and Forgiveness, acquired its name after the decision was made *not* to name it The Uncertain Baptist Church, The Uncertain Methodist Church, or even the Church of Uncertain Love and Forgiveness.

Townspeople claim that their city limits road sign is the most stolen in the state--and they seem secretly proud of the fact.

But how did the name come about? While filling out the town's incorporation papers, the group in charge couldn't agree on a name, so they put down "uncertain," intending to supply the name later. The state of Texas took them at their word.

Uncertain lies twenty-five miles northeast of the city of Marshall, Texas, long famed for its Ellis Pottery. The definitely named towns of Fair Play, Texas, and Plain Dealing, Louisiana, are nearby.

VIRGIN, UTAH

It was in 1858 that pioneers settled down near a beautiful clear river in southwestern Utah. Grateful for its purity, they called the river Virgin and named their new community after the river.

A few minutes after midnight on January 1, 1989, an earthen dike broke just south of town, and a twelve-foot wall of water from the Virgin River was unleashed on the nearby community of St. George. Homes and apartments were flooded; fifteen hundred residents were evacuated. No one was injured, but confusion resulted when some people thought the civil defense sirens were part of the New Year's celebration.

Nearly 140 years have passed since the unpredictable river and the nearby town received their virtuous names. Zion National Park now lies next door to Virgin and its two hundred residents. Oil fields and towns with the rougher names of Hurricane and Gunlock are nearby.

Oh, yes. The Virgin River is no longer virgin, having acquired some murkiness along the way.

Things change.

WATCH HILL, RHODE ISLAND

Watch Hill has lived up to its name for at least three hundred years.

A persistent local legend recounts the wistful tale of a Narragansett Indian maiden who watched from her vantage point on the hill as her sweetheart paddled with other braves across the Block Island Sound. Though the maiden watched until her death, none of the Indians returned from their battle with enemies encountered across the water at the spot now known as Montauk Point.

Later, in the British colonial period, the highest point on the same hill was the site of a watchtower during the French and Indian War. Soon after, during our own battles to gain independence from British rule, American Revolutionary soldiers kept their vigil from the same lookout atop Watch Hill.

Today the community is a section of Westerly, Rhode

119

Island. Its residents watch their numbers swell fivefold each summer as their locale is transformed into an affluent summer resort similar to nearby Newport.

WATERPROOF, LOUISIANA

Lying very close to the west bank of the lazy, snake-like Mississippi River is the small community of Waterproof. Civil War history abounds throughout the area. Vicksburg, Mississippi, home of the Vicksburg National Military Park, lies forty-five miles up the river; Natchez, Mississippi is twenty miles to the south.

Pioneers, traveling by wagon on the old Texas Road Trail and on flatboats floating down the river, arrived at this location around the year 1830. The rich delta soil was a welcome sight to these wanderers, and they envisioned rich farmlands producing abundant crops.

One of the first settlers, Mr. Abner Smalley, was standing along the river bank as he was greeted by a riverboat captain passing by.

"Well, Abner," the captain shouted. "I see you are waterproof."

This so pleased Mr. Smalley that he then and there decided to call his land holdings Waterproof.

But the name of Waterproof was overly optimistic. The town had to be moved twice due to the flooding of the river. To make the name even more of a misnomer, the present site of Waterproof has had several floods that covered the entire town to a depth of three to four feet.

Waterproof was incorporated in 1872. By the first decade of the twentieth century, in response to frequent spring floods, a twenty-five-foot levee was built as a defense against the river's moods. Now Waterproof lives up to its name. Most years.

WHIGVILLE, CONNECTICUT

More than a sporting rivalry was involved in one game of wicket in west-central Connecticut back in 1845. The year before, Democrat James Polk had won the presidential election, climaxing a spirited campaign. He defeated Henry Clay, a leader of the Whig party--a party that was gaining strength in the 1840s and later evolved into the Republican party.

During this era the game of wicket, related to today's sport of cricket, was becoming popular. Teams formed to challenge one another.

Two teams from the Bristol area were scheduled to compete on the nation's birthday, July 4, 1845. The captain of one team, Thomas Lowrey, asked rival team captain Philo Curtis what his group was called. Curtis answered by painting "Polksville" along the length of his bat.

"Then mine will be called Whigville," retorted Lowrey, obviously a staunch supporter of Clay and the Whig party. The settlement of Whigville had found a name.

More than 140 years later, Connecticut folks play baseball rather than wicket on the Fourth of July, Polksville has turned into Edgewood, and the community of Whigville is a part of Burlington--but Americans still savor their political passions.

WINNER, SOUTH DAKOTA

It was 1909, and rivalries could be bitter in southern South Dakota.

In this Pine Ridge area of the Great Plains west of the Missouri River, Lamro, the county seat, and a hostile unnamed neighboring settlement were platted only two miles apart. The railroad tipped the scale, laying tracks right through the second town. Most of Lamro's residents deserted it for the luckier community, which triumphantly proclaimed itself Winner.

To add insult to injury, the courthouse records were stolen from Lamro and brought to Winner, which was declared the county seat of Tripp County in 1910.

Winner now boasts a population of thirty-seven hundred Winners, and Lamro has disappeared entirely. Winner's neighbors these days are Ideal, Reliance, Hidden Timber, Bonesteel, and Rosebud, the latter located on the Rosebud Indian Reservation.

YANKEETOWN, FLORIDA

How many towns in the United States have been christened through outright ridicule?

In the early 1920s Mr. A. F. Knott and a party of fewer than ten left Gary, Indiana, and traveled by automobile until they reached a spot on the Gulf Coast of central Florida. They decided to set up camp and proceeded to build two shanties. They then devoted their time to the excellent hunting and fishing the region afforded.

Knott returned to Indiana each year to urge others to try his corner of Florida in the autumn. These converts, drawn by Knott's stories of the abundant hunting, fishing, and coastal beauty, would arrive at nearby Dunnellon by train. For transportation to the camping area, they hitched a ride with the star route carrier, Mr. Hugh Coleman.

Coleman became somewhat disgruntled with the increasing numbers of "Yankees" arriving from the North. Reluctantly, he agreed to transport these "interlopers" to the place he had dubbed Yankeetown. (If he had used the more common term, the town might have ended up being called "Damn Yankeetown"!)

Incorporated by the Florida Legislature on December 15, 1925, Yankeetown has a present-day population of eight hundred to one thousand.

In 1960 the people of Yankeetown found themselves in a heated presidential political debate with opionated folks from nearby Crackertown. They decided to settle their sometimes passionate arguments with a straw vote to be held several weeks prior to the real election.

The two towns received state and national TV and radio coverage. Votes were taken in each town, and each sent a motorcade to meet halfway on State Route 40 to record the result. The gathering of more than one hundred vehicles, fire trucks, and horses resulted in a traffic jam--something never seen in the area before nor since. A lighthearted holiday atmosphere prevailed during the vote and tabulation.

For the record, John Kennedy carried Crackertown, Richard Nixon outpolled his opponent in Yankeetown, and Nixon won the overall straw vote. But Crackertown prevailed in the real election, with Kennedy the victor.

ZZYZX, CALIFORNIA

Zzyzx (pronounced Zye-zix) is located a few miles northwest of the Devils Playground in the desert of southeastern California. The East Mojave National Scenic Area is nearby, and the town of Baker lies ten miles to the northeast. Interstate 15, linking Los Angeles and Las Vegas, runs four miles north of Zzyzx.

This area has seen it all: numerous primitive cultures, an eighteenth-century Spanish priestly traveler, American explorers and trappers including Kit Carson, a midnineteenth-century freight carrier who used camels as his pack animals, a federal army outpost of Indian fighters, a commercial rest stop for travelers during the final quarter of the century, an early twentieth-century railway station, and a short-lived colony established by the founder of the Jehovah's Witnesses. But "Doc" Springer topped them all.

Prior to 1944 the area was known as Soda Springs, and some still call it that because of the presence of numerous salt deposits. With 1944 came Curtis and Helen Springer from Hollywood. Doc Springer's first impression was that the area was a mosquito swamp. Nevertheless, he rolled up his sleeves and went to work, building a health resort and tax-exempt community church and religious retreat.

The unusual name, Zzyzx, was coined by this eccentric entrepreneur. Springer invented Zzyzx to have the "last word." He wanted to have a name at the end of the alphabet, and he felt that this name would assure him the last spot on any list anyone could devise.

His plan was to supply the paying guests with a special diet, "health treatments," the climate of the desert, and religion. Alcoholics were invited, it is said, to "dry out."

Over the next few years, Springer, on twelve thousand acres of public land, set up a sixty-room hotel, a rabbit farm, and a goat dairy that produced milk, cheese, and ice cream. He installed mud and mineral baths, a power plant, a print shop, a radio station, an airstrip, a swimming pool in the shape of a cross, wood- and metal-working shops, a fountain, and a boat dock.

In addition, Springer set up a laboratory to produce several dozen "beauty" preparations and "health" foods. He gave them names like zychrystals, zymud, and NCF (nerve cell food). The NCF contained more than 55 percent invert sugar, with a price of ten dollars a can. Springer also produced a "cure-it-yourself" hemorrhoid kit priced at twenty-five dollars each. This kit and his NCF preparation earned him a six-month sentence in the county jail. All of Springer's products were sold on radio stations throughout America through tapes pro- duced at Zzyzx. Springer never named a price for the concoctions in the radio advertisements. Instead, he sprinkled religion into his sales pitch, telling audience members that their donation was "between you and God." The money rolled in to Zzyzx. It is estimated that Doc Springer's enterprises brought in an average of $500 thousand each year.

Springer envisioned castles, waterways, and golf courses on his land. He did build a tree-lined road called "Boulevard of Dreams" and another called "Sun- rise Boulevard"--both of which led nowhere. He claimed to have planted seven thousand shade trees, two thou- sand palm trees, and four thousand flowering bushes. For his guests, he offered hot mineral baths--but heated the water himself.

Although the first of many court cases against him came in 1968, the seeds of Springer's problems had been sown at the very beginning of his sojourn in the desert. Upon moving onto public land in 1944, he had filed mining claims on the property. He had stated to the U.S.

Government Bureau of Land Management that he was going to "mine and/or harvest minerals." It was on this fraudulent mining claim that the BLM went after him in court several decades later.

Prior to the BLM suit, the American Medical Association had brought action against Springer for the medical "potents" he was offering on his radio shows. Some impressed spectators referred to him as the "King of the Quacks."

The Internal Revenue Service finally joined the chase, charging Springer with tax evasion. The Food and Drug Administration wasn't far behind with charges of false advertising. The many court cases kept Springer busy for years.

The BLM had the last word as far as Doc Springer was concerned. They won their court case because, under an 1872 law, Springer was not legitimately mining. (The mining of money from the gullible did not qualify.) He was evicted from the 12,800-acre spread in April 1974. Actually, Springer's last vehicle left shortly before the arrival of the BLM representatives.

Two years later, the BLM agreed to allow the California State University System to use the property and abandoned buildings as a field research station for desert studies. Today the two organizations cooperate in the management of the Desert Studies Center. During the less kindly seasons of summer and winter, only Robert E. Fulton, manager of the center, his wife, and their two sons are in residence at Zzyzx. During the spring and fall seasons, when the Mojave Desert is more hospitable for study, the center is host to students and faculty from numerous institutions and organizations. A different vision, one of science and scholarship, now enlivens these 12,800 acres located at the end of the alphabet.

SOURCES

Accord, Massachusetts	Lawrence Corthell
Aladdin, Wyoming	Judy Brengle
Amigo, West Virginia	Postmaster, Amigo
Aromas, California	Jan B. Ingram
Bad Axe, Michigan	Joseph M. Dean
Ballplay, Alabama	Joe Barnes
Bath, Indiana	Anon., Bath
Bimble, Kentucky	T. Adkins
Blessing, Texas	A. B. Price
Boulevard, California	Anne A. Woempner
Brothers, Oregon	Ramsays Stage Stop, Brothers
Sisters, Oregon	Sisters Chamber of Commerce
Busy, Kentucky	Anon., Busy
Captain Cook, Hawaii	Honannai Sita
Cashtown, Pennsylvania	C. F. Singley
Climax, Minnesota	Kathy Evenson
Cowpens, South Carolina	Wilhelmina Dearybury
Cyclone, Pennsylvania	Mary Burton
Dames Quarter, Maryland	Anon., Dames Quarter
Death Valley, California	Michele Moore and Sandi Moore
Defiance, Iowa	Postmaster, Defiance
Detour, Maryland	Miss Wilhelm and Postmaster, Detour
Devils Elbow, Missouri	Postmaster, Devils Elbow
Drytown, California	C. R. Kaffer
Embarrass, Wisconsin	Lucille Radthe
Fiddletown, California	Anon., Fiddletown
Freedom, Maine	Ellen Letourneau
Freedom, Wyoming	Postmaster, Freedom
Friendship, Tennessee	City of Friendship and Bank of Friendship
Gas, Kansas	L. W. Walters
George, Washington	Mrs. Charles E. Brown
Harmony, California	David C. Sprague and Tom Rousseve
Hell, Michigan	Milton E. Charboneau and Rose Ley
Home, Kansas	Jim Schramm Jr.

Hoot Owl, Oklahoma	Hoot Owl City Hall and William Bradley
Hope, New Jersey	Hester H. Hartung
Horseheads, New York	Postmaster, Horseheads
Ink, Arkansas	Anon., Mena, Arkansas
Ixonia, Wisconsin	Delores Saeger
Jackpot, Nevada	Carl Hayden
Jet, Oklahoma	Bonnie Stanley
Jot 'Em Down, Texas	Anon., Paris, Texas
King and Queen Court House, Virginia	Anon.,King and Queen Court House
Knockemstiff, Ohio	Anon., Chillicothe, Ohio
Letter Gap, West Virginia	Anon., Letter Gap
Loco, Texas	Mrs. Cecil Mills
Lulu, Florida	Alton Gillen and Delores Schmid
Magnet, Nebraska	Delwyn Norman
Marathon, Florida	Robert Norton and Danny Williams
Marys Igloo, Arkansas	Johanna Ahlowaluk
Midnight, Mississippi	Mary S. Robertson
Muck City, Alabama	Thomas B. Warren
Nalcrest, Florida	Edwin J. Hughes
Needmore, Pennsylvania	Anon., Needmore
Nocatee, Florida	Visit to town
Oil City, Pennsylvania	O. C. Chambers
Oil City, Wisconsin	Irma Olson
Old Glory, Texas	Anon., Old Glory
Orient, Maine	Anon., Orient
Parachute, Colorado	Phil Wheelock
Parade, South Dakota	Elsie F. Wright
Paradox, Colorado	Robert Proctor
Peerless, Montana	L. M. Puckett
Picnic, Florida	Man in Tampa restaurant
Pie, West Virginia	Anon., Pie
Pie Town, New Mexico	Nita Larronde
Pigeon, West Virginia	Kanawha County Public Library
Podunk, Massachusetts	Howard Drake and Virginia Hebert
Porcupine, South Dakota	Anon., Porcupine

Possum Trot, Kentucky	George W. and Margueretta Lofton
Pure Air, Missouri	Joe Broseghini
Reform, Alabama	Pat Whiat
Rescue, Virginia	Lillian W. Huntley
Revloc, Pennsylvania	Arvel G. Mash
Rifle, Colorado	Phil Wheelock
Rough and Ready, California	Constance Baer
Round O, South Carolina	P. Utsey
Sandwich, New Hampshire	Bertha Gotshall
Skull Valley, Arizona	Mrs. Mary Kakal
Slapout, Oklahoma	Judith B. Lemmons
Sleepy Eye, Minnesota	Judy Beech
Smut Eye, Alabama	Charles T. Tussell
Stalwart, Michigan	Anon., Stalwart
Star, Idaho	Ada Ayres Smith
Sunspot, New Mexico	John W. Evans and John Cornett
Sweet Lips, Tennessee	Kenneth Davis
Taintsville, Florida	Anon., Oviedo, Florida
Telephone, Texas	Anon., Telephone
Ten Sleep, Wyoming	Wyoma Pyle, Gail Anderson, and Henry Webster
Tightwad, Missouri	Tom Skaggs and Connie Easter
Tin Cup, Colorado	Gunnison County Chamber of Commerce
Toad Hop, Indiana	Reverend Art Lindsey
Tropic, Utah	Mrs. Ella Adair
Turkey Scratch, Arkansas	A. B. Thompson Jr.
Twain Harte, California	Twain Harte Chamber of Commerce
Two Dot, Montana	Donna Haass and Daloris Olson
Two Egg, Florida	Mrs. Carey L. Lawrence and Attaway Barnes
Uncertain, Texas	Anon., Uncertain
Virgin, Utah	Yvonne Wilcox
Watch Hill, Rhode Island	Edgar Carroll
Waterproof, Louisiana	Charles Rushing Jr.
Whigville, Connecticut	George Moffitt
Winner, South Dakota	Harvey V. Jorgensen